GUMBO FOR THE BLACK WOMAN'S SOUL
Stories of Resilience, Triumph, and the Power of Sisterhood

By
LeAnne Dolce

Copyright © 2024 by Wake Up Happy Sis Inc.

All rights reserved. No part of this publication may be reproduced, distributed, or transmitted in any form or by any means, including photocopying, recording, or other electronic or mechanical methods, without the prior written permission of the publisher, except in the case of brief quotations embodied in critical reviews and certain other noncommercial uses permitted by copyright law. For permission requests, please contact the publisher.

Published by Wake Up Happy Sis inc.
600 Bronner Bros Way SW, Suite Y532, Atlanta, GA 30310
https://pubs.wakeuphappysis.com
support@wakeuphappysis.com

First Edition

ISBN (paperback): 978-0-9823328-6-3

Library of Congress Control Number: 2024943417

Book Cover Design by LeAnne Dolce

Printed in the United States of America

DISCLAIMER

The stories presented in "Gumbo for the Black Woman's Soul" are the personal accounts and experiences of the contributing authors. While we expect and trust that each author has provided an accurate and truthful representation of their life events, the publisher cannot guarantee the absolute accuracy of every detail.

The publisher, Wake Up Happy Sis Inc., has not independently verified the information contained within these stories and therefore does not assume responsibility for any inaccuracies, errors, or omissions that may be present. The views, opinions, and experiences expressed by the authors are their own and do not necessarily reflect the views or positions of the publisher.

By sharing their stories, the contributing authors have courageously opened a window into their lives, offering readers a glimpse into their personal journeys of resilience, growth, and transformation. We honor and respect the authenticity of their voices and the bravery it takes to share one's truth.

As you read these powerful accounts, please keep in mind that memory is subjective, and the recounting of life events may be influenced by the passage of time, personal perspective, and the profound impact of the experiences themselves.

Our goal in publishing this anthology is to create a space for Black women's voices to be heard, celebrated, and validated. We stand by our contributing authors and the integrity of their stories, recognizing that their experiences, as shared, have the power to inspire, heal, and uplift readers on their own journeys of self-discovery and empowerment.

To my resilient sisters around the globe,

This book is dedicated to you – the warriors, the dreamers, the survivors. To every Black woman who has ever felt the weight of the world on her shoulders, who has fought tooth and nail for her place in the sun, who has dared to hope for a better tomorrow.

I see you, sis. I see your struggles, your scars, your indomitable spirit. I see the way you rise, time and time again, like a phoenix from the ashes of your past. I see the fire in your eyes, the determination in your step, the love in your heart that refuses to be extinguished.

Your journey has not been easy. You've weathered storms that would have broken lesser souls. You've faced adversity, discrimination, and pain that no one should ever have to endure. But through it all, you've held your head high. You've kept pushing, kept believing, kept reaching for the light.

And I'm here to tell you, sis – that light is real. There IS a pot of gold at the end of the rainbow, waiting for you to claim it. There IS a life beyond the struggle, a future filled with joy, peace, and purpose. You may not see it yet, but it's there, just beyond the horizon.

So keep going. Keep fighting. Keep believing in yourself and your dreams. You are stronger than you know, more powerful than you can imagine. You are a force of nature, a goddess in human form.

This book is a reminder that you are not alone, that there are sisters all around the world standing with you, cheering you on, holding space for your healing.

May these stories be a balm for your soul, a light in the darkness, a compass pointing you toward your true north. May they remind you of your own inherent worth, your own boundless potential.

You are loved, sis. You are seen. You are enough, just as you are.

Keep shining. Keep rising. Keep reaching for the stars.

Table of Contents

Foreward vii

Introduction xi

Chapter 1 Why Settle: Questioning Constraints to Unleash Your Commercial Creativity (Aviella Aloha) 1

Chapter 2 Solace in Security: Crafting Your Sanctuary of Wealth from Creative Talent (Aviella Aloha) 9

Chapter 3 If I Dare: Tap into the Power of the Persistent Woman (Jennifer Dukes) 17

Chapter 4 Seasons Beneath the Scars: Confidently Harvesting Happiness by Transforming Pain into Strength (Elaine Tatum) 25

Chapter 5 Sparking the Phoenix: Transcending Trials to Triumph in the Quest for Self-Discovery (Sheran Duncan) 35

Chapter 6 Just My Imagination: A Life Reimagined from Silent Turmoil to Roaring Tranquility (Melissa Andrewin) 43

Chapter 7 The Art of Mindful Rebuilding: Practices for Healing the Mind, Body, and Spirit After Trauma (Roberta Bell) 51

Chapter 8 Her Life Rewritten: Crafting Your Comeback Story with Courage (Nannette Palmore) 61

Chapter 9 From Nothing to Something: A True Story of God's Redemption (Samantha Dantzler) 69

Chapter 10 The Chameleon's Quest: Rising Above the Labels to Live Your Truth (Tamara Sidney) 77

Chapter 11 Breaking the Silence: Confronting the Shadows of Abuse (Stephanie Walker) 87

About LeAnne Dolce 97

Reader's Guide/ Discussion Questions 100

Endorsements 103

Join the Wake Up Happy Sis Academy 104

"I can be changed by what happens to me. But I refuse to be reduced by it."

Maya Angelou

FOREWARD

Sisters, let me be clear: this anthology you're holding isn't just a book. It's a revolution bound in paper and ink, a battle cry echoing through generations of silence. I'm Dr. Evelyn Bethune, and I'm here to tell you that "Gumbo for the Black Woman's Soul" is about to shake you to your core and rebuild you stronger than ever.

Now, you might be wondering, "Who is this woman, and why should I listen to her?" Fair question. I'm the founder of History in the Making Coaching Network, Inc. and CEO of The Dr. Mary McLeod Bethune Family Legacy, Inc. But more than that, I'm a Black woman who's seen the ugly underbelly of America's promises and decided to flip the script. The work of my grandmother, Dr. Mary McLeod Bethune, taught me that education and resilience are our superpowers. I was only 3 years old when she passed away so my personal recollection of her is that of a grandmother. But I grew up in the amazing light of her legacy, and let me tell you, the women in these pages? They're straight-up superheroes.

Let's break it down. This anthology is like a perfectly seasoned gumbo – rich, complex, and guaranteed to stick to your ribs. Each story is an ingredient, carefully chosen and lovingly prepared. But make no mistake, this ain't your grandma's feel-good recipe book. These stories will burn your mouth with truth and leave you hungry for justice.

As I devoured these pages, I was transported back to the kitchens of my youth. You know the scene – women gathered around a bubbling pot, laughter and tears mixing with the steam. That's where the real magic happened. That's where we alchemized our pain into power, our struggles into strength. And that's exactly what this book does.

Take Aviella Gray's chapter, "Why Settle." Sister came out swinging, challenging every lie we've been fed about our worth. Then there's Elaine Tatum's "Seasons Beneath the Scars," a soul-stirring journey that'll have you examining your own wounds and finding beauty in the healing.

But let me tell you about Stephanie Walker's "Breaking the Silence." Her story hit me like a freight train, exposing the shadows we've been taught to hide in. By speaking her truth, she's creating space for all of us to step into the light. And isn't that what we need? To break these chains of silence that have been choking us for generations.

Now, I know some of y'all are thinking, "But Dr. Bethune, we're strong Black women. We don't need help." Let me stop you right there. That "strong Black woman" narrative? It's a trap, designed to keep us carrying the weight of the world without complaint. Roberta Bell's chapter on mindful rebuilding and Samantha Dantzler's journey from "Nothing to Something" are here to remind you that true strength lies in vulnerability, in asking for help, in prioritizing your own damn well-being.

Listen, I've been in the trenches of education and personal development long enough to know that knowledge is power. But these stories? They're showing us that our lived experiences are just as valuable as any textbook. They're proof that no matter where you start, no matter what hand life deals you, you've got the power to rewrite your story. It also shows how very important it is to tell our own stories through our own voices.

But here's the real tea – this book isn't just about individual triumph. It's about sisterhood. In a world hellbent on pitting us against each other, these stories are a rallying cry for unity. They remind us that when we lift each other up, we all rise.

Now, let me put on my Dr. Mary McLeod Bethune's granddaughter hat for a second. My grandmother used to say, "The true worth of a race must be measured by the character of its womanhood." Looking at the women in these pages, I'd say we're priceless. Their courage, their wisdom, their relentless pursuit of growth – it's a testament to the strength that runs in our veins.

But don't get it twisted. This book isn't here to make you feel good and send you on your way. It's a call to action. It's challenging you to dig deep, confront your own demons, and step boldly into your light. It's daring you to break cycles, redefine success on your own terms, and create a life so authentic and joy-filled it scares the status quo.

To every sister picking up this book: what you're holding is more than paper and ink. It's a treasure map to your own power, a mirror that'll show you your true beauty, scars and all. Let these stories feed your soul, challenge your mind, and ignite a fire in your spirit.

And to LeAnne Dolce and all the brave women who bared their souls in these pages: I see you. I honor you. Your vulnerability is your superpower. You're carrying the torch passed down by every strong Black woman who came before us, lighting the way for generations to come.

As we feast on this literary gumbo, remember this: your story, your voice, your experience – that's the secret ingredient the world is hungry for. Share it. Let it nourish and heal and transform.

May this book be your wake-up call, your comfort in the storm, your reminder that you are descended from women who turned pain into power and despair into determination. May it inspire you to stand tall, dream big, and lift as you climb.

In the words of my grandmother, "If we have the courage and tenacity of our forebears, who stood firmly like a rock against the lash of slavery, we shall find a way to do for our day what they did for theirs." This book is a testament to that courage and tenacity. It is a beacon of hope, a celebration of our resilience, and a powerful affirmation of the transformative power of sisterhood.

Now, sisters, it's time to rise. The world is waiting for your magic. Let's show them what Black women can do when we stand together, unbreakable and unstoppable.

Dr. Evelyn Bethune
Founder, History in the Making Coaching Network, Inc.
CEO, The Dr. Mary McLeod Bethune Family Legacy, Inc.

INTRODUCTION

Hey Sis, it's your girl LeAnne here, and I am so excited to welcome you to this incredible journey we're about to embark on together. This isn't just another book; it's a voyage into the very heart of what it means to be a Black woman in this world. It's a testament to our strength, our resilience, and our unbreakable spirit. It's a celebration of the magic that happens when we come together, share our stories, and lift each other up.

When I started Wake Up Happy, Sis!, it was more than just a business venture. It was a calling, a soul-deep knowing that I had to create a space where my sisters could come to heal, to grow, to find their joy again. You see, I've been where you are. I've felt the weight of the world on my shoulders, the pressure to be everything to everyone, to keep pushing even when I was running on empty. I've been through the fire of depression, obesity, and overwhelming stress. There were days when I didn't think I could take another step.

But here's the thing, sis. I didn't just survive those dark times; I learned to thrive. I discovered that when I started putting myself first; when I made my happiness and well-being a priority, everything else began to fall into place. It wasn't easy, and it didn't happen overnight, but day by day, I began to heal. I began to rediscover the vibrant, powerful, joyful woman I was always meant to be.

And that's what I want for you. I want you to wake up every morning feeling excited about your life, knowing that you have the strength to handle whatever comes your way. I want you to look in the mirror and see the queen that you are, to treat yourself with the love and compassion you so freely give to others. I want you to know, deep in your bones, that you are worthy of happiness, of peace, of a life that sets your soul on fire.

That's why I poured my heart and soul into creating this anthology. I wanted to bring together a chorus of voices, a sisterhood of warriors who have been through the trenches and come out the other side. These are women who have faced unimaginable challenges, who have been knocked down time and time again, but who have always found the strength to get back up. They are living proof that no matter how dark the night is, joy always comes in the morning.

As you read these stories, I want you to see yourself in these pages. I want you to feel the power of their words washing over you, filling you up with the courage and the determination to keep going, to keep reaching for your dreams. I want you to know that you are not alone, that there is a whole community of sisters out here who see you, who hear you, who are cheering you on every step of the way.

We're going to dive deep into this anthology, sis. We're going to talk about the things that society tells us we're not supposed to talk about. We're going to shine a light on the pain, the trauma, the struggles that we've been carrying for far too long. But more importantly, we're going to celebrate the triumphs, the breakthroughs, and the moments of pure, unbridled joy that make this journey so worthwhile.

You're going to meet women like A. Gray, who learned to break free from the chains of settling and step into her true power. You'll be inspired by Jennifer's story of daring to be her authentic self, no matter what the world might say. You'll find solace in E. Tatum's journey of healing, of finding the beauty and the strength in her scars. And you'll be ignited by the phoenix rising from the ashes in S. Duncan's tale of unshakable resilience.

But that's just the beginning. With every turn of the page, you'll encounter another sister who will touch your heart, who will make you laugh, who will move you to tears. You'll discover that your story is woven into the tapestry of their lives, that your pain and your joy are echoed in the collective experience of Black womanhood.

And through it all, I'll be right here with you, sis. I'll be your guide, your cheerleader, your sister in the struggle and in the triumph. Because that's what Wake Up Happy, Sis! is all about. It's about creating a community of love, support, and understanding. It's about giving you the tools and the resources you need to prioritize your happiness, heal from your past, and step into the glorious future that awaits you.

So take a deep breath, sis. Grab a cup of tea, find a cozy spot, and get ready to embark on a journey that will change your life. You're about to discover the extraordinary power that lies within you, the unshakable strength that has been forged in the fires of your experiences. You're about to find your tribe, your soul sisters, the women who will lift you up and remind you of your magic when you've forgotten it yourself.

This is more than just a book, sis. This is a movement, a revolution, a reclamation of our joy, our power, and our unbreakable spirit. It's a love letter to every Black woman who has ever felt alone, unseen, or unworthy. It's a rallying cry, a call to rise up and claim the life we deserve.

Because here's the truth, sis. You are a force of nature. You are a goddess, a warrior, a queen. You have everything you need to create a life that sets your soul ablaze with passion and purpose. And with every page of this anthology, you'll be reminded of that truth, over and over again.

So let's dive in, together. Let's laugh, cry, and heal as one. Let's celebrate the magic and the resilience of Black womanhood. Let's wake up happy, sis, and show the world what we're made of.

This is just the beginning of your journey, and I am so honored to be a part of it. Welcome to the sisterhood, welcome to the movement, and welcome to the rest of your life. Let's do this, together.

With all my love and sisterhood,

LeAnne Dolce
Your Chief Self-Love Officer
Wake Up Happy, Sis!

CHAPTER 1

WHY SETTLE: QUESTIONING CONSTRAINTS TO UNLEASH YOUR COMMERCIAL CREATIVITY

Aviella Aloha

"Through courage, clarity, and conviction, harness the power of transformation, authoring your own tale of triumph and self-realization."

In the quiet of dawn, where the promise of a new day melds with the residue of night, I sit and reflect on a journey that began in darkness but led to light. My story, a testament to the resilience of the human spirit, unfolds from an unlikely beginning—a childhood marred by unjust confinement within the stark, cold walls of a mental health facility. There, amidst adversity and suppression, the seeds of my future were sown.

Betrayed by the very systems designed to protect, I learned at a tender age that survival meant forging my own path, questioning every constraint, and dismantling the oppressive structures that sought to define and confine me. The realization dawned harsh and clear: I was not merely to survive but to thrive, to transform pain into power and loss into profound triumph. This principle—that through courage, clarity, and conviction, we can harness the power of transformation and author our own tales of triumph and self-realization—would become the guiding light on my journey.

I was just twelve, a bright student with dreams bigger than the confines of the mental health facility where I found myself trapped. My journey to that cold, unwelcoming place started on an ordinary school day and turned into a nightmare. A severe allergic reaction to pollen exposed me to a system ready to exploit my vulnerability rather than aid my recovery. The school nurse, who should have been my advocate, instead set in motion a chain of events that would rob me of my childhood and my trust in those meant to protect me.

Taken from school to what I was misled to believe was a hospital for my allergies, I was instead incarcerated in a mental health ward. This marked the beginning of an eight-month ordeal where my rights as a human and a child were stripped away under the guise of treatment. The facility was a prison, and my crime was simply being in the wrong place at the wrong time, with a system eager to label a young girl with hay fever as mentally unstable.

The days turned into weeks and months of resistance. I was subjected to treatments I didn't need and medications I refused to take. They labeled me "incorrigible" because I fought against their control. I questioned everything, trusting my instincts over their authority, which only deepened their resolve to break my spirit. But with each attempt to mold me into submission, my resolve to define my own destiny grew stronger. I was sculpting my own identity with clarity and conviction, carving out who I truly was amidst the detritus of who they wanted me to be.

The nights were haunted by the presence of a roommate who believed herself to be a vampire, her delusions fueled by the very medications meant to "cure" her. My days were a battle against a system determined to strip me of my autonomy, my meals reduced to peanut butter and crackers as punishment for my refusal to comply with their pharmaceutical regime. Yet, even in the face of this oppression, I held fast to the belief that my mind and body were my own, and no authority had the right to dictate my thoughts or actions.

The challenges I faced extended beyond the walls of the mental health facility. I navigated the harsh realities of the Annie Malone group home and endured intermittent stints in foster care and other mental institutions. The feeling of being a pawn in a larger game played by indifferent hands was palpable. Every "emergency placement" echoed the harsh truth—my father's refusal to claim me, his daughter, relegating me to a day in a jail cell awaiting another spot in the facility I had vowed never to return to. It was a stark reminder of my unworthiness in his eyes and the system's cold clutch.

Despite the oppressive environment, it was here, in the darkest moments, that the foundation of my future self was laid. I learned the value of personal fortitude, the importance of questioning authority, and the undeniable power of self-advocacy. I learned that sometimes, to change your circumstances, you must first endure and then engage the system on its terms, only to subvert them for your emancipation. I was overcoming the villain of vagueness, sharpening my sword of specificity to slice through the confusion and clarify my goals.

When I was finally released, I returned to a home that no longer felt like one. The stark realization that I was on my own was both terrifying and liberating. With nothing but a teddy bear, a bus pass, and a profound distrust in the systems that failed me, I stepped into independence at the tender age of twelve. I embraced my epic, becoming the author of my own tale.

Amid this turmoil, I found sanctuary at a good friend's house. His mother, a woman whose name whimsically echoed that of a grasshopper, became my unexpected savior. She welcomed me not just into her home but into her heart, offering me the kind of maternal care and tough love I had sorely missed. "You might not have come from my body, but you're my daughter all the same," she'd say with a stern yet loving look. She provided food, shelter, and occasionally, the threat of discipline if I strayed too far from the path she believed I could tread—one leading to safety and success.

Despite being technically "on the run," evading the persistent gaze of authorities, I was adamant about continuing my education. The need for progress, for feeling forward movement in a life filled with uncertainties, was my guiding light. I navigated daily challenges—from dodging gang recruiters who saw in my desperation an opportunity to exploit, to warding off predators who preyed on vulnerable girls like me. My so-called play brothers, fiercely protective yet wild, provided a buffer between me and the darker elements of street life.

It would be years before I learned the full truth of what happened during those lost months. In a moment of vulnerability, my mother revealed the depths of the betrayal. The very system that had torn me from her arms had also exploited her, forcing her to pay for the "privilege" of my incarceration. The classes they mandated her to take, the fees they extracted, all while I languished in their "care." The weight of this revelation was staggering, but it also served to further fuel my determination to rise above the injustices of my past.

This transformation was neither swift nor easy. It demanded everything of me: every shred of courage, every bit of clarity in vision, and an unwavering conviction in my values and capabilities. These were the pillars upon which I rebuilt my life, leading to the eventual triumph not just in business, but in crafting a life marked by freedom and defined on my own terms.

I first tasted entrepreneurship at the age of 14, starting with a simple yet profound venture—selling candy. This was no ordinary business; it was a rebellion against the narrative written for me by others, a claim to autonomy, and a step toward financial independence. From those early days, each transaction was a lesson in commerce and courage, each customer interaction a step towards mastering my destiny. I was rallying my resources, summoning support for my quest.

As I navigated the complexities of growing a business, I embraced education and personal development as my allies. I delved into books on philosophy, strategy, and entrepreneurship, each page-turning the gears of my mind, expanding my worldview, and fortifying my resolve. My business grew from a solo endeavor into a thriving enterprise, mirroring my own transformation from a victim of circumstances to a victor of my own making. I was mapping my milestones, envisioning victory, and setting my sights on success's summit.

In the safety of relationships built on trust and mutual respect, I discovered the true power of rallying resources. My journey was not just about surviving but about thriving, about transforming the support I received into a ladder that would help me climb to new heights. I learned to make choices that skewed towards the better, if not the best possible outcomes, relying solely on my judgment. This independence of thought, this refusal to succumb to the 'group think' that could have easily swallowed me whole, I count among my most treasured traits.

Now, as I share my journey with you, it is not just to recount my victories but to offer you the roadmap I used to achieve them. Here are the strategies that were pivotal in my journey, and how you can apply them to your own:

- Clarity of Vision: Know what you want and chart your course with precision. Just as I did, define your goals clearly and let them guide you through the fog of uncertainty.

- Rally Your Resources: You are not alone. Seek out mentors, form alliances, and engage with communities that align with your vision. Just as allies bolstered my journey, let them fuel yours.

- Celebrate Each Milestone: Recognize and celebrate each victory, no matter how small. These milestones are beacons on your path to greater achievements, just as they were on mine.

- Embrace Continuous Learning: Never stop learning. Education is the weapon with which you can carve a path through adversity and illuminate your journey toward success.

- Lead with Courage: In the face of challenges, remember that courage is not the absence of fear, but the triumph over it. Let your bravery guide you as it did me.

As you turn these pages, see them as more than just a story; they are an invitation to you to embark on your own journey of transformation. Let the lessons here light your path, and may you find in them the strength to rewrite your own epic. Through courage, clarity, and conviction, harness the power of transformation, authoring your own tale of triumph and self-realization. This is your strategic saga, your way to victory. Embrace it.

My journey didn't end with my escape from the facility. It was merely the beginning of a lifelong odyssey of healing, growth, and self-discovery. The path has been winding, the challenges numerous, but with each step, I have come closer to the truth of who I am and the limitless potential that resides within me. And now, I extend my hand to you, inviting you to walk this path alongside me. Together, let us question the constraints that seek to confine us, rally the resources that will sustain us, and celebrate each milestone that marks our progress. Let us embrace the power of our own transformative tales and rise, triumphant, as the authors of our most extraordinary lives.

CHAPTER 2

SOLACE IN SECURITY: CRAFTING YOUR SANCTUARY OF WEALTH FROM CREATIVE TALENT

Aviella Aloha

In harmonious collaboration, diverse talents dance, creating a symphony of success grander than solitary efforts could ever compose.

When you hear the title "Solace in Security: Crafting Your Sanctuary of Wealth from Creative Talent," what visions come to mind? Picture a serene oasis where calm waters meet the vibrant, flourishing land, a place where your creative spirit is not only nurtured but celebrated—a sanctuary where every grain of sand tells a story of resilience and growth.

In the spirit of Aloha, how can we find solace in our financial journeys? How can we transform our unique talents into fortresses of security that not only shelter us from the storms but also enrich the soil of our future generations? This title isn't just a phrase; it's an invitation to embark on a journey of deep personal discovery and profound financial empowerment.

Imagine a world where your brand of creativity is the key to unlocking a life of abundance and peace. Here, your skills and passions are not just hobbies; they are the bedrock of a wealth strategy that embraces the Aloha spirit—always love over hate, always. It's about finding the courage to weave your talents into a tapestry of wealth that wraps you and your loved ones in warmth and security.

This sanctuary of wealth isn't built from bricks and mortar but from the bold strokes of your dreams and the vibrant colors of your determination. Here, each moment of financial learning and each decision made in the spirit of love and clarity is a brushstroke on the masterpiece of your life's canvas.

So, close your eyes and breathe in the essence of this sanctuary. With each breath, feel the peace that comes from knowing you are on your path to financial solace. And as you exhale, ask yourself, "In the spirit of Aloha, how can I craft my sanctuary of wealth from my creative talent?"

My journey of entrepreneurship and continued education was not just about discovery—it was about empowerment. In 2006, as I graduated from Missouri Western University with a B.S. in Travel & Tourism Management and an undocumented minor in marketing and small business, I felt like I was ready to conquer the world. Inspired by the idea of adventure and guided by the wisdom of Nelson Mandela, who said, "Education is the most powerful weapon which you can use to change the world," I embarked on an internship that whisked me away to the magical realms of Walt Disney World Resorts in Orlando, FL.

By 2007, I found myself navigating the pristine waters of Hawaii with Norwegian Cruise Line America, much like Moana on her daring ocean journey, exploring uncharted waters with resilience. However, the tide turned abruptly in 2008. In the aftermath of the stock market crash, like a scene from "The Pursuit of Happiness," I was laid off and found myself without a home, living out of a tiny camping tent on the picturesque but challenging terrains of Maui.

As Sara Bareilles would sing, "Show me how big your brave is," I found my courage at a local craft fair bustling with life and opportunity. It was there, among the colorful tents and vibrant entrepreneurs, that I realized my own potential to craft a future from the ashes of my past. My prior training in cosmetology, though prematurely ended by an allergic reaction to the chemical mixtures used for nail services, became the unexpected foundation for my new venture.

In this vibrant marketplace, no one was offering hair braiding—a skill I possessed and could monetize. Echoing the strategic mindset of a chess grandmaster, I set up my booth, not just offering a service but creating a brand. Island Braids by Taz became an Urban-n-Island consortium. I expanded my empire by crafting beauty products from scratch—oils, creams, jars of butter—each jar a testament to my journey from hardship to hope.

For over 13 years, this business flourished, turning every challenge into a stepping stone, much like Oprah Winfrey's ascent from poverty to power, reminding us that we can "Turn your wounds into wisdom." The freedom this venture afforded me was intoxicating; I traveled, lived comfortably, and savored life's pleasures.

Until December 2019 when the "Vid" a worldwide pandemic breakout without warning.

COVID-19, an infectious disease caused by the SARS-CoV-2 virus shut the entire world down for months affecting my mental health balance. Forcing me to cash in my SEP IRA and my Roth IRA with a huge balance reduction penalty for early withdrawal. If I only new then, what I know now! For some reason, my black woman-owned small business did not qualify for any financial relief until the last week of May 2020. August 8, 2023, when the island of Maui faced a profound tragedy—the devastating wildfires that swept through communities, claiming the lives of many: children, women, men, and grandparents. There isn't one Maui resident who didn't get affected either directly or indirectly.

This heartbreaking event served as a stark reminder of the fragility of life and the importance of securing not just our financial future but also cherishing the present moment with our loved ones. As we reflect on this loss, let us pause and breathe in deeply, feeling the gift of life flowing through us. This moment of gratitude reminds us that while we strive to build sanctuaries of wealth, the truest wealth we hold is our health and the well-being of those we love. It compels us to think deeply about how we generate our income and the impact of our choices on our community and environment. Let this poignant memory drive us to create lives filled with meaning and purpose, ensuring that our pursuits honor those we've lost and celebrate the life we still have the privilege to enjoy.

Somehow, in my devastation of the loss of business, resources, and relationships with a cloudy impaired vision in my spirit the whisper of ambition spoke again, posing a powerful question that would redefine my path: "What if I could rebuild myself in a way that would allow me to make more money without working more?"

This question launched my quest into the world of financial literacy, transforming every dollar earned into a soldier in my army of wealth, diligently working to secure my financial future. I was not just surviving; I was thriving, crafting a sanctuary of wealth that was both a fortress and a testament to my creative spirit.

As I stand today, enriched not just in wealth but in wisdom, I extend an invitation to you. Reflect on your own journey and consider, how resolving past pains changes your approach to money and wealth. For me, embracing entrepreneurship was not merely a professional choice but a profound step toward healing and self-actualization.

From the shadows of a tent on Maui to the spotlight of success, my story is a beacon for all who dare to dream. In the words of Sara Bareilles, "I wonder what would happen if you say what you wanna say and let the words fall out." So I ask you, are you ready to let your bravery show and transform your talents into a legacy of wealth?

As our tale of transformation draws to a close, let the harmony of our shared journey resonate within you. "Solace in Security" isn't merely a story; it's a compass for navigating the vast seas of financial uncertainty with the heart of an explorer.

In the spirit of Aloha, how can we turn these lessons into stepping stones for your journey? Here's how you can chart your course:

- **Seek Knowledge as Treasure**: Dive into the depths of financial education like an ocean explorer seeks hidden treasures. Engage in workshops, devour books, and navigate through webinars to uncover the gems of financial wisdom.
- **Craft Your Map**: With a vision as clear as the Maui skies, sketch out your life plan. Align this map with your deepest values, needs, and talents. Each line drawn should guide you closer to the sanctuary of your dreams.
- **Set Sail with Purpose**: Launch your journey not on a whim but with deliberate actions. Whether it's saving a fraction of your earnings or embarking on a venture that speaks to your soul, let every action reflect your dedication to your financial haven.

- **Navigate and Adjust**: The path to tranquility, like the ocean, changes its tides. Regularly assess your financial health and adjust your sails as needed. Be as adaptable as the sailors of old, who read the stars and seas to find their way.
- **Share Your Voyage**: Stories of the sea are best told around a warm fire, inspiring others to embark on their own adventures. Share your journey of financial empowerment with others, igniting a chain of inspiration that lights up countless paths.

As you forge ahead, remember that crafting your sanctuary of wealth is a dynamic voyage, demanding creativity, courage, and commitment. In the spirit of Aloha, how will you make each day a step towards weaving your financial dreams into reality?

Let this narrative not only guide you but also serve as a beacon, illuminating your path to a future where you are not merely secure but profoundly at peace and fulfilled. Embrace this voyage, for it is uniquely yours, and let the spirit of Aloha light your way to a sanctuary built from your own indomitable spirit and creative talents.

About Aviella Aloha

Aviella Aloha, a visionary leader and entrepreneur based on the vibrant island of Maui, specializes in transforming financial education into a conduit for creative and purpose-driven wealth creation. With a background steeped in travel, tourism management, financial education instruction, and an undocumented passion for marketing and small business growth, Aviella has carved a niche in helping individuals, particularly women, and people of color, navigate the complexities of financial independence through innovative learning experiences.

Founder of the Purpose Driven Wealth Network, Aviella not only champions the philosophy of 'Always Love Over Hate Always' but also integrates this ethos into every aspect of her business. Her educational programs and personal coaching are not just about financial literacy; they are about crafting a lifestyle that harmonizes personal fulfillment with financial stability.

In her journey from adversity to abundance, Aviella has learned that the truest form of security comes from understanding and leveraging one's creative talents. She believes in empowering her clients to create their own sanctuaries of wealth, not through conventional paths, but through personalized strategies that resonate with their individual stories and aspirations.

Are you ready to transform your financial destiny? Discover your unique pathway to purpose-driven wealth. Take Aviella's insightful quiz today and start crafting your personalized blueprint for financial freedom. As a thank you for purchasing the book, you get to attend our next Purpose Driven Prosperity 5-DAY CHALLENGE for FREE when you sign-up after taking the quiz. Aloha!

https://www.startthequiz.com

CONNECT WITH AVIELLA

FB: @Purpose Driven Wealth Creator

IG: @Purpose_Driven_Wealth_Network

CHAPTER 3

IF I DARE:
TAP INTO THE POWER OF THE PERSISTENT WOMAN

Jennifer Dukes

In the symphony of existence, the tenacious spirit is a flute - its melody ignited by mindfulness, self-reflection, and unwavering belief.

In the scorching summer of 1980, amidst the upheaval of a family move from Chicago to Thiensville, Wisconsin, a young Jennifer stood on the precipice of an extraordinary journey—one that would forge her spirit in the fires of adversity and sculpt her into a beacon of resilience.

Thiensville, with its predominantly white neighborhood, stood in stark contrast to the vibrant, close-knit community Jennifer had known in Chicago. Here, she encountered isolation and the bitter sting of racial slurs. Yet, even as the shadows of prejudice loomed, a light flickered in the form of Jennifer's mother—a wellspring of strength and wisdom.

It was in the crucible of third grade that Jennifer's path took a pivotal turn. When a male classmate hurled a racial epithet at her, she responded with a fierce uppercut, a physical retaliation that left his nose bleeding. But her mother's words in the aftermath struck a deeper chord: "You can't hit everyone just because you don't like what they said to you." This moment marked the dawn of a powerful realization for Jennifer—that her words could be mightier than her fists, that she could wield truth and conviction to dismantle prejudice and assert her worth.

As Jennifer navigated the complexities of her teenage years, she found herself at a crossroads during a pivotal classroom debate. In this heated discussion about cultural heritage and individual destiny, Jennifer's voice rose above the fray, infused with the wisdom of her mother's teachings and the fire of her own aspirations. Her eloquence and conviction not only won her the debate but also earned her the respect and admiration of her peers and teachers.

This triumph was more than a fleeting victory; it was a mirror that reflected Jennifer's evolution from a reactive child to a self-assured, articulate advocate for her own path. It illuminated the transformative power of embracing one's story—not just the shimmering highlights, but also the shadows of struggle and complexity.

For Jennifer, this self-reflection became a catalyst for growth, a way to transmute pain into purpose. By acknowledging and learning from her experiences, she began to sculpt a narrative of resilience, one that would resonate with the collective journey of countless women standing at the threshold of their own potential.

As Jennifer stepped into the corporate world, she found herself in an environment where her voice often seemed muffled by the authoritative tones of seasoned professionals. It was a recurring struggle, a discordant note that threatened to drown out her own melody.

But Jennifer had learned to listen to life's cacophony with a discerning ear, to find the spaces between the notes where her own voice could rise and resonate. She began to see her challenges not as immovable barriers, but as steppingstones to growth and self-discovery.

This shift in perspective was a testament to Jennifer's evolving resilience—a quality forged not in a single, defining moment, but in the accumulation of daily acts of courage and persistence. By learning to find harmony amidst the discord, she demonstrated that struggles are not merely obstacles to endure, but opportunities to cultivate strength and self-understanding.

In a particularly turbulent chapter of her journey, as Jennifer grappled with career stagnation and personal setbacks, she discovered the transformative power of mindfulness. Attending a workshop on meditation and mindfulness marked a turning point, offering her a path to navigate the tempests of life with renewed clarity and intention.

Mindfulness became a steadfast companion on Jennifer's path, teaching her to observe her thoughts and emotions without judgment and to respond rather than react to life's provocations. Each moment of presence became a tesserae in the mosaic of her self-understanding, revealing patterns and possibilities that had once been obscured by the haze of reactivity.

This practice of mindfulness empowered Jennifer to reclaim the authorship of her own narrative. No longer a passive participant buffeted by life's capricious winds, she learned to steer her course with intention and grace. By anchoring herself in the present, she discovered a deep well of inner strength, a reservoir of resilience that would sustain her through the trials and triumphs to come.

As Jennifer stepped into the role of community leader, she confronted the intricacies of social dynamics and the gaps in her own understanding. Rather than shrinking from this challenge, she embarked on a quest for knowledge, traversing the winding paths of formal education and the rich terrain of lived experience.

Each book, seminar, and conversation with a mentor became a luminous thread in the tapestry of her wisdom. But it was in the application of this knowledge, in the daily alchemy of turning insight into action, that Jennifer found true empowerment. By weaving learning into the fabric of her leadership, she developed the flexibility to adapt, the foresight to anticipate, and the influence to inspire.

This dedication to lifelong learning became a compass on Jennifer's journey, guiding her through the labyrinthine complexities of personal and professional growth. It illuminated the interconnectedness of her experiences, revealing how each twist and turn on her path contributed to a larger story of resilience and transformation.

At the heart of Jennifer's extraordinary journey beats a steadfast rhythm—the unwavering conviction in her own potential. This self-belief, nurtured through trials and triumphs, has been the guiding light illuminating her path, the eternal flame that transforms obstacles into opportunities and challenges into chances for growth.

Jennifer's self-conviction is not a product of ego, but a hard-won understanding of her own worth, forged in the crucible of self-reflection and tempered by the wisdom of experience. It is a quiet strength, a deep certainty that no matter what storms may come, she has the resilience to weather them, the adaptability to learn from them, and the tenacity to emerge stronger.

This unshakable belief in oneself is the beacon that can guide each of us through the uncertainties and upheavals of our own journeys. By tending to the flame of our self-conviction, by daring to trust in our own potential even when the path ahead seems shrouded in darkness, we tap into a wellspring of resilience and transformative power.

As Jennifer's story so luminously illustrates, this self-belief is not a destination to be reached but a constant companion to be nurtured. It is the steady light that guides us through the darkest nights of doubt and the anchoring force that keeps us rooted in our truth as we navigate the turbulent waters of change.

Dear reader, as you stand on the threshold of your own journey, carry the beacon of Jennifer's story in your heart. Let it illuminate the pathways of possibility before you, casting light on the hidden strengths and untapped potential within.

Remember that resilience is not a singular destination but a daily practice, a commitment to meet each challenge with courage and each setback with self-compassion. It is in the consistent, quiet moments of showing up for ourselves that we weave the tapestry of our own transformation.

Embrace the power of your own narrative, the unique story that has shaped you, and the chapters yet unwritten. Dare to reflect on your journey with honesty and grace, to find the glimmers of growth amidst the shadows of struggle. For it is in owning our stories that we reclaim the power to shape our destinies.

Like Jennifer, trust in the alchemy of your words and the conviction of your beliefs. Let your voice rise in the face of adversity, not with the force of aggression but with the unwavering strength of your truth. Believe in the transformative potential of your own wisdom, and let that belief guide your steps.

Above all, remember that within you burns an inextinguishable flame, a beacon of resilience that can illuminate even the darkest of paths. Nurture this light with the fuel of self-reflection, self-care, and self-belief. Surround yourself with those who fan your flames and seek out the knowledge and experiences that help you burn brighter.

For when you dare to embrace the power of the persistent woman, when you trust in the brilliance of your own light, you become an unstoppable force for transformation—in your own life and in the lives of all those you touch.

So rise, dear reader. Rise with the radiance of your own conviction, the tenacity of your own spirit. Rise to illuminate the world with the singular brilliance of your resilience. For in daring to shine, you ignite the potential for all of us to rise together, to create a world where every woman's story is a beacon of possibility and every voice a catalyst for change.

In the tapestry of our collective resilience, your thread is vital, your light essential. Dare to weave your story with the bold strokes of self-belief, to illuminate the path for yourself and for the women who will follow in your footsteps.

For when we dare to rise together, when we embrace the power of our persistence and the radiance of our shared light, there is no darkness we cannot transform, no challenge we cannot overcome, no dream we cannot make manifest.

This is the legacy of the persistent woman—a world illuminated by the brilliance of our resilience, a future shaped by the courage of our conviction. So let us rise, together, and dare to shine.

About Jennifer Dukes

Jennifer Dukes aka J. Eileen hails from the southeast by way of the Midwest. She is a poignant writer who captures the essence of the human experience. Jennifer is the proud pet parent of two overly indulged house cats, Big Baby and Boss Lady. In her spare time, she enjoys crocheting and reading.

CHAPTER 4

SEASONS BENEATH THE SCARS: CONFIDENTLY HARVESTING HAPPINESS BY TRANSFORMING PAIN INTO STRENGTH

Elaine Tatum

In the quiet dawn of self-awareness, hold the mirror to my soul, and transmute shadows into light for an empowered transformation.

As dawn's first light brushes the horizon, a soft glow spills through my window, casting long, gentle shadows across the room. This quiet moment marks the beginning of my day, just as my journey of self-discovery began in the quietude of introspection. I am Elaine Tatum, a woman carved from the trials of my past, a survivor shaped by each tempest faced and each adversity embraced.

Reflecting on my life, I see a tapestry woven with threads of resilience and colored by the hues of hard-won wisdom. Born three generations removed from slavery, into a world still shackled by the remnants of old prejudices, my voice—strong and assertive—often clashed with the stifling expectations of a society not ready to hear it. In my family, "children were seen and not heard", "what goes on in this house stays in this house", a mantra that muffled my thoughts and bound my spirit. Yet, it was this very suppression that kindled the flame of self-awareness within me, a flame that would eventually light my path to empowerment.

From a young age, I stood out as different, 'troublesome,' because I saw visions of things yet to come—visions that frightened my family because they invariably were accurate. These glimpses into the future, dismissed by many, were the early signs of my unique perspective, a gift that I would only come to appreciate and understand much later. Feeling like the black sheep of the family from whom I yearned for love, contributed to me becoming depression-prone and unable to see my worth. My parents were great providers materially, but to hear "I love you" was only a dream. Being a child, I didn't know people display their love the best way they know how, so I had a lot. My brother displayed animosity that I could not understand which crushed my spirit and a daily beating was normal.

My journey through personal relationships mirrored the oppressive dynamics I had known as a child. Each relationship, imbued with the shadows of my father's narcissism and betrayal (which he developed from his mom's twin sister who abused him emotionally) became a battleground where old wounds were reopened, and the scars of my past were etched deeper into my soul. I experienced domestic violence so severe that I ran out of my apartment naked into the street. God sent an angel who gave me refuge. My case changed the legal system for NYC's order of protection for women who were not married to, lived with, or had children by the abuser. It was not until my battle with fourth-stage breast cancer, during which I endured not only the physical ravages of the disease but also the torment of a partner who was an emotional/spiritual vampire (narcissist) who belittled my struggles, cheating, gaslighting, etc. that I realized the cycle of pain I had been reliving. I remember one day he came in and said "this relationship is going to be my way or no way", so I said "bye". But when he did not leave I thought, foolishly, that he was willing to work on building a bond, when in reality he was strategically working on breaking me down.

Lying awake at night, the echoes of harsh words ringing in my ears, I reached a breaking point—a moment of profound clarity. "Enough is enough," I told myself, crying tears of resolve mixed with the pain of revelation. This epiphany was not just about recognizing the toxic patterns I had perpetuated but about acknowledging my part in them. It was time to break free, to transform my pain into a source of strength because I had always been downplaying my self-worth to be loved and accepted.

After a gut-wrenching, tear-jerking cry, (the one that put you to sleep), I awakened to a tear-soaked pillow, curled in a fetal position, clutching a teddy bear. "How did I get here again? What am I doing wrong?" The realization hit me like a thunderbolt: I had not learned my lessons and was trapped in a vicious cycle that had plagued me my entire life. But this last betrayal was the final straw because it was an amalgamation of all the past unlearned lessons plus new stuff. Wow, this was deep. At that moment, I made a vow: "Never again! This will never happen to me again. I am worth more than this, I deserve better, I am enough, and I will not take it anymore." That's when I decided to embark on a journey of self-discovery, to uncover who I truly was beneath the layers of pain and suppression.

Armed with the wisdom of poets like Maya Angelou, who's "Still I Rise" resonated with the core of my being, I began to see my experiences not as burdens but as stepping stones. I prayed earnestly and embraced stoicism (which helped me navigate the tumultuous waters of my emotions and experiences). I learned to set boundaries and stand on them, a practice that, while perceived by some as harsh, was essential for my peace and well-being.

At the age of 29, I read a book about the turning points in our lives (which everyone goes through approximately every 8-10 yrs) and realized I had not met any of my goals. Depressed, I attempted suicide by taking 750 pills. As I ingested the pills, I kept apologizing to God, knowing I would miss heaven. Miraculously, I woke up. "Damn, you still here!". Determined to end my life, I cut my wrists, making sure to hit the arteries. My friend, (who I had forgotten had a key to my home), found me. The doctors couldn't understand how I survived because I had done everything right to accomplish my goal. They stitched my wrists and pumped me for 6 hours. Through therapy, reconnecting with that same friend who encouraged me lovingly, and revisiting books that had kept me years previously, I started to piece together the mosaic of my identity. Each fragment, each shard of broken dreams, was carefully examined and placed into the framework of the new person I was/am becoming. This was not just healing; it was a rebirth.

In this journey of self-discovery, I confronted the masks I had worn—the roles of mother, survivor, and mediator (how do you do that and are so broken?) I had always been able to help others, just not seeing I needed to help myself.—and began to excavate the core of my authentic self. I nurtured the seeds of my genuine desires and dreams, allowing them to blossom in the light of self-awareness. This quest for authenticity required me to wield the spade of curiosity, digging through the layers of conformity to uncover the roots of my true self.

I came to understand that my desperation for love had led me to become a people-pleasing, codependent wreck. Despite recognizing red flags, I allowed others to mistreat, emotionally abuse, and disrespect me. It was a painful but necessary realization: I had to be honest with myself and accept what I had allowed all these years. Being three generations removed from slavery, my boldness, visions, and dreams were deemed unacceptable, and attempts to beat them out of me daily were instilled. The journey from victim to victor had begun, and it was both exhilarating and painful.

Delving deep into my soul, peeling the onion, I recognized the patterns that had shaped me. For decades, I repeated the same cycles in relationships, seeking validation where it was least available. It took profound introspection, often during the quiet moments of chemotherapy, to see that these patterns were not inevitabilities but choices—choices that could be changed with awareness and courage.

In the mirror of reflection, I confronted the woman I had become, acknowledging every flaw and every strength. I learned to embrace my shadows, the parts of myself that had lingered in the dark, as teachers rather than enemies. By shining a light on these aspects, I began to integrate them, transforming vulnerabilities into wellsprings of resilience.

Crafting the mosaic of change required setting clear, achievable goals aligned with my deepest values and aspirations. Each goal became a piece of the mosaic, intentionally placed to create a coherent and beautiful whole. I sought God and other resources and support—strong relationships, therapeutic practices, and continuous education—to fortify the overall structure of my transformation.

My 35-year battle with drug addiction added another layer of complexity to my journey. The road to recovery was paved with countless obstacles and setbacks, each one threatening to derail my progress. Yet, it was through the crucible of addiction that I discovered the depths of my own strength. With each day of sobriety, I proved to myself that I was capable of overcoming even the most daunting challenges.

As a mother, my journey of self-discovery took on an added dimension. I wanted to be a guiding light for my children, to break the cycle of pain and oppression that had been passed down through generations. By openly sharing my struggles and triumphs, I hoped to instill in them the belief that they, too, could rise above their circumstances and create a life of their own design.

Throughout my odyssey of self-discovery, I learned to harness the power of prayer, daily reflection (stoicism), and meditation. These practices became my anchors, grounding me in the present moment and providing clarity amidst the chaos. By carving out sacred spaces for introspection, I have cultivated a deeper understanding of my own needs and desires, allowing me to make choices that align with my authentic self.

On this path to self-love, I first had to forgive myself, then the people I had allowed to mishandle me, and accept myself fully, both my strengths and weaknesses. I took concrete steps to nurture my well-being. I listened to affirmations throughout the night, wrote them on sticky notes, and placed them around the house. I penned love letters to myself, and woke up each morning with a smile and a "Good morning, beautiful." I disciplined myself, created boundaries for myself and others, and navigated my days with intention, fueled by daily meditation and prayer.

My focus shifted to making myself happy, and in doing so, I discovered a joy and peace I had never known before.

When you don't learn your lessons, you will keep going around in circles until you do. That's God's love. He doesn't want you to be lost. I had to hit rock bottom to get my life back. I am now living a life I never thought I would have and am so happy I never gave up. Never, ever, ever give up on yourself!

Today, I have shared my journey, I did so not to dwell on the pain but to celebrate the triumph over it. This chapter of my life, much like the dawn that greets me each morning, is filled with light—a light that I now know was always within me, waiting to be acknowledged and embraced. It is a light I wish to share with you, the reader, as you navigate your own journey of self-discovery.

Let this be your invitation to transformation:

- **Embrace the dawn of your self-awareness.** Recognize that the first step to change is being honest, accepting, and understanding yourself deeply without judgment. By shining a light on your inner world, you gain the power to reshape your outer reality.

- **See the beauty in your scars.** Your wounds, both visible and invisible, are not marks of shame but testaments to your resilience. Embrace them as part of your story, and allow them to fuel your growth rather than hinder it.

- **Recognize your pain as a catalyst for growth.** The challenges you face, no matter how daunting, hold within them the seeds of your transformation. By reframing your pain as an opportunity for learning and evolution, you reclaim your power and redirect your path.

- **Reclaim your power and redefine your destiny.** You are the author of your life story, and you have the power to shape its narrative. Embrace yourself, trust in your strength, accept your weakness (challenges), and boldly step into the life you desire and deserve.

With each word you read, imagine yourself walking alongside me, stepping out of the shadows of your past and into the light of your future. Let each sentence strengthen your resolve to rise, to heal, and to transform your own life.

As we continue, let us delve deeper into the essence of self-reflection, exploring the mirror of our souls and the truths that shape our existence. Join me as we uncover the authenticity beneath the roles we play and the masks we wear, finding the courage to be our truest selves.

About Elaine Tatum

Elaine Tatum is a working retiree, mother, and grandmother. Elaine is a certified grief, crisis intervention, substance abuse counselor. She enjoys working at Care Net for pregnant teenagers, counseling them of their rights and options about the pregnancy. This includes testing, housing, education and career path plans and more. Sister, Inc was another facility where she received great satisfaction in helping women who were recently paroled and had nowhere to go. There, she facilitated the 12-step program, helped them enroll in school, took them on job interviews, taught them how to dress for success and instilled self-esteem, confidence and a desire to move forward in their lives. She currently volunteers with Guardian Ad Litem, Hospice care and other organizations. Feeding the homeless is also one of her passions, however her greatest passion is encouraging women into taking back authority over their lives.

Connect with Elaine

FB: @MeyersElaine

IG: @KRAZFX

CHAPTER 5

SPARKING THE PHOENIX: TRANSCENDING TRIALS TO TRIUMPH IN THE QUEST FOR SELF-DISCOVERY

Sheran Duncan

Through self-discovery's embers, fan your potential, for true power arises from the ashen wisdom of experience and self-knowing.

In the depths of Sheran Duncan's being, whispers of her past and present dance together, guiding her on a profound journey of self-discovery. With each step, she unearths the precious treasures buried within her essence - resilience, wisdom, and an unbreakable spirit forged in the fires of adversity. Sheran's story is a testament to the indomitable human spirit, a shining beacon illuminating the path from pain to purpose. Her journey is a symphony of survival, a melody of hope rising from the ashes of despair.

Sheran's path has been far from easy. Abuse in its many insidious forms - sexual, physical, mental, emotional, and financial - marred her early life. The trauma train barreled through her world, its passengers bonded by shared childhood atrocities that felt normal only to them. Broken objects and shattered dreams littered the landscape of her youth. She was told not to do this and not to do that, her dreams of a happy childhood crushed under the weight of the abuse she endured. The scars on her womb and the wounds embedded in her mind bore witness to the unspeakable horrors she faced. The nights were filled with silent screams, the days with a numbness that threatened to consume her. She felt like a shell of a person, a mere shadow of the vibrant soul she once was.

Yet even amidst the pain, Sheran held tight to her inner light. She learned to transmute her suffering into strength, to find beauty in the broken pieces of her life. Like the Gullah Geechee ancestors who wove sweetgrass baskets, Sheran began to weave the fragments of her shattered self into something beautiful and resilient. She discovered that within her wounds lay the seeds of her wisdom, that her scars were not marks of shame, but badges of survival. Like copper filled with impurities, she allowed the fires of her trials to burn away the dross, leaving behind a shining, resilient spirit.

Sheran became a miner of her own memories, sifting through the ashes of her past to uncover glimmers of wisdom. Each hardship endured held a lesson; each moment of despair concealed a seed of hope. She recalled the nights spent silently crying, the days spent walking through hell hand-in-hand with her abuser. She remembered the times she thought she couldn't go on, the moments when death seemed kinder than life. Yet something within her refused to be extinguished, a stubborn flame that whispered, "Keep going." Through quiet introspection, she began to recognize the patterns woven through her life - threads of courage, perseverance, and an indomitable will to rise.

Balance became Sheran's artform as she learned to tend to the hearth of her own harmony. She discovered the power of the pause, the necessity of replenishing her spirit amidst the chaos of life. She learned to be gentle with herself, forgive her own perceived failings, and celebrate her triumphs, no matter how small. She discovered that true equilibrium is not static perfection but a dynamic dance- a give-and-take between self-care and service, rest and resilience. By listening to the needs of her body and soul, Sheran crafted rituals of replenishment, moments of sacred pause amidst the whirl of life.

With this newfound balance came the wisdom to set boundaries - protective rings of self-respect encircling the bonfire of Sheran's spirit. No longer would she allow others to trespass upon her well-being. 'No' became her shield, her declaration of self-love, her refusal to be a verbal punching bag or a receptacle for others' pain. She learned that setting boundaries was not selfish, but self-preservation, a necessary act of love for the precious being she was. 'No' became her wand, dispelling undue burdens and affirming her worth. Each boundary set was a declaration of love for herself, a promise to safeguard the sanctity of her being.

Like the mythical Phoenix, Sheran began to rise from the embers of her experiences. Each trial endured became fuel for her ascent, propelling her towards a future of her own design. She gathered the coals of her past, the searing memories of abuse and betrayal, and used them to ignite the flames of her transformation. She realized that her past did not define her and that she could rewrite her story from this moment forward. She gathered the lessons of her past, breathing life into them with the winds of determination, setting her spirit ablaze with purpose.

Sheran's journey became a forge, where the hammer of her will meet the anvil of her reality. With each strike, she shaped her path, scripting a codex of deliberate action and unwavering intent. No longer a prisoner of her past, she became the architect of her future. She began to dream again, to envision a life of joy, love, and fulfillment. She became the creator of her own destiny, painting her world in the vibrant hues of hope and possibility. No longer a passenger on the trauma train, she became the conductor of her own destiny, steering towards a horizon of healing and growth.

Through the crucible of her experiences, Sheran emerged a woman transformed. Where once she couldn't bear to look at her own reflection, now she eagerly greets the sun each morning, marveling at the priceless, handcrafted, purposeful being staring back at her. She sees a warrior, a survivor, a woman of immeasurable strength and beauty. She sees a masterpiece, an exquisite tapestry woven from the threads of her triumphs and tears. Through her metamorphosis, Sheran uncovered a profound truth: her legacy was not merely something to leave behind, but a beacon to construct throughout her life. With every act of resilience, every word of wisdom shared, she wove a luminous tapestry - a testament to the transformative power of embracing one's whole self.

Sheran's story is a clarion call, a battle cry for all those who have been silenced, shattered, and left to reassemble themselves in the shadows. It is a love letter to the wounded, a testament to the unbreakable nature of the human spirit. It whispers, "You, too, can rise." Her journey reminds us that our trials, when alchemized by introspection and resolve, can become the very wings that lift us toward redemption.

In the echoes of Sheran's empowered existence, we find a call to forge our own paths, to meet our shadows with compassion, and to tend to the flames of our resilience. We are reminded that we are the blacksmiths of our own souls, wielding the hammer of our choices and the anvil of our experiences. We are reminded that we are not merely survivors, but thrivers, capable of crafting lives of purpose and passion from the rubble of our pasts. We are reminded that self-discovery is not a destination, but a lifelong dance - a sacred movement between the darkness of our past and the light of our becoming.

So let us, like Sheran, become the alchemists of our own lives. Let us transmute the lead of our pain into the gold of our purpose. Let us take up the hammer of our own courage, meeting our lives at the anvil of transformation. Let us sift through the ashes of our experiences, gathering the embers of wisdom they hold. And let us, like Sheran, rise - again and again - from the fires of our past, forever reaching toward the light of our most radiant selves. For in the end, it is not the trials we endure that define us, but the phoenix we become in the process of rising. Let us spread our wings and soar, painting the skies with the brilliant hues of our resilient spirits. Let us become the beacons of hope we once so desperately sought, lighting the way for others to rise from their own ashes and claim their rightful place in the world.

To those who find themselves in their own trials, know that you are not alone. Know that your pain, though it may feel all-consuming, is not permanent. Like Sheran, you have the power to transmute your suffering into strength, your wounds into wisdom. Trust in the resilience of your spirit, in the unbreakable nature of your soul.

Seek out the support of others, for we were never meant to weather life's storms alone. Surround yourself with those who see your light, even when you cannot. Allow their love and belief in you to be the mirror that reflects your own radiance back to you.

Be patient with yourself as you navigate the path of healing. Remember that growth is not linear and that setbacks are not failures, but opportunities for deeper learning and self-compassion. Celebrate every victory, no matter how small, for each one is a testament to your courage and determination.

Above all, never lose sight of the truth that you are worthy of love, respect, and joy. Your past may have shaped you, but it does not define you. You are not the sum of your scars, but the totality of your triumphs. You are a living, breathing miracle, a phoenix in the making.

So rise, dear one. Rise from the ashes of your pain and spread your wings wide. Let your story be a beacon of hope, your voice a clarion call of resilience. Let your journey inspire others to reclaim their own power, to rewrite their narratives from victim to victor.

And as you rise, remember that you carry within you the strength of all those who have risen before you. You are the legacy of the survivors, the dreamers, the phoenixes who refused to be reduced to ashes. You are the proof that no matter how dark the night, the dawn always comes.

Rise, phoenix, rise. The world is waiting for the gift of your light.

About Sheran Duncan

Sheran Duncan is a wife, mother, sister, grandmother and friend that has been blessed with the opportunity to witness the miracle of life through community and family. She has been equipped to guide and nurture her children and grandchildren, as well as a communal healer by serving her community as a Certified Full Spectrum Doula. A calling that brings her immense joy and fulfillment. Sheran also heralds as an activist in the womaness movement to empower women and advocate for their rights and equality.

She deeply believes that every woman has a unique strength and potential within her, and it is our communal duty to help each one recognize and unleash it. The end result would help create a society that values and uplifts all its members to live an equal and equitable life regardless of gender. In 2014, Sheran founded Happiitears Inc, a mission that resonated deeply from within. Happiitears is purposed to helping women find happiness in every moment, to appreciate the beauty and lessons that come with both the joys and challenges of life to truly grow and find fulfillment. Sheran believes "We are all connected, and our individual journeys contribute to the collective tapestry of humanity. Every step we take, every struggle we face, and every triumph we celebrate has a purpose and significance. It is through sharing our stories and supporting one another that we can create a ripple effect of positive change in our communities and beyond leaving #nothingwasted.

Connect with Sheran

FB @sheranlangfordduncan

IG @sheranlangfordduncan

CHAPTER 6

JUST MY IMAGINATION: A LIFE REIMAGINED FROM SILENT TURMOIL TO ROARING TRANQUILITY

Melissa Andrewin

The compass of my heart, always pointing to my true North, guides me through the wild lands of self-discovery towards the serene shores of inner truth.

Growing up, I didn't have the essential things a child needed for healthy development - stability, love, guidance, and protection. I was the last of my mother's four children. She was a sweet, soft-spoken lady from Mississippi, who I loved very much. She wasn't much of a disciplinarian, but I believed she did the best she could as a single parent working multiple jobs to barely make ends meet.

My father was in and out of my life, never providing the guidance I needed and craved from him as a young girl. I often wished another man would be revealed as my real father, saving me from the nomadic, unstable lifestyle my soul screamed to get out of. I loved my siblings, but we all had issues. Through them, I witnessed the consequences of poor choices and the absence of positive role models. My older sister's promiscuity led to early motherhood, while my brother's drinking habit and abusive behavior towards me until I was 19 years old left deep emotional scars. Watching their struggles, I knew I wanted a different path for myself, and I found inspiration in my oldest sister's hard work and perseverance. Her example showed me that it was possible to rise above our circumstances and create a more comfortable life.

The pain of my childhood ran deep, leaving scars that I carried into adulthood. The lack of stability and protection left me feeling vulnerable and unsure of my place in the world. I longed for the love and guidance that every child deserved, but instead, I found myself navigating a minefield of emotional turmoil. The constant moving, the absence of a reliable father figure, and the dysfunction within my family all contributed to a sense of unease that permeated my every waking moment.

As a daydreamer, I could see myself in happier, safer situations. I felt that if I pursued life's formula of getting an education, a good job, practicing healthy habits, and growing myself in a spiritual belief system, I'd have a better life one day. Little did I know that the trauma of my childhood would follow me into adulthood, influencing my choices and relationships.

At 19, I met my ex-husband in community college. Jumping from the fire of my turbulent childhood into the frying pan of an emotionally abusive relationship, I thought I had found the stability, love, and protection I craved. But the emotional abuse persisted, as we both grappled with our own unresolved traumas. I sought to deal with mine, while he ignored his and blamed mine for ruining our relationship.

We had two daughters, eight years apart, and I poured my heart into being a working mother, wife, and homemaker. I went to school and worked for local government agencies, priding myself on adorning our home with Black images that represented our culture. My girls were clean, cared for, and involved in various sports and social, educational, and church activities. My heart was set on making my family work. I didn't want to contribute to the negative statistics of failed Black marriages and families.

But the childhood trauma my ex and I both experienced made it difficult for us to really love, understand, and care for one another. He was my best friend, but our fights were like World War III at times, full of gaslighting, blame, and lack of personal responsibility. We didn't realize the detrimental impact those disputes had on our daughters. We separated for several years before eventually divorcing, and the ultimate circumstance that prompted our actual divorce was extremely heartbreaking, severing all chances of us having any type of relationship in the foreseeable future. That part hurt the most.

The life-changing moment that finally gave me the strength to leave my ex-husband came when I realized the toll our toxic relationship was taking on our daughters. Feeling the pain and confusion exuding from them, I knew I had to break the cycle of trauma and dysfunction. I couldn't bear the thought of my girls growing up believing that love meant enduring abuse and neglecting their own well-being. It was a moment of clarity that shook me to my core, and I knew I had to find the courage to walk away, not just for myself, but for the future of my daughters.

For three years, I grieved the loss of my marriage, feeling like I was dying slowly. My health deteriorated, and I turned to drinking and smoking (weed) at every available opportunity. I was a walking emotional time bomb, and my relationship with my daughters suffered as I grieved. I said and did some pretty hurtful things to them that I'm not proud of while they were experiencing their own pain during that time.

I was determined to lift myself out of that state of being. Over time, I realized how much I made my ex-husband the biggest star of MY story! I committed to lots of therapy and self-care, and now I am in a place of forgiveness – forgiving all those in my life who've hurt me, as well as receiving forgiveness from those I've hurt, namely my daughters. I committed to especially forgiving my ex-husband because I can't move forward in MY life carrying those heavy chains of anger and grief. Instead, I'm appreciative of the road of self-discovery and self-love that all those relationships led me on. God has great things in store for me, and I'm excited about what He has to show me.

Through this journey, I've learned the importance of acknowledging my feelings and validating my experiences. My pain, fears, and doubts are real and deserving of attention, and allowing myself to feel these emotions without judgment is a natural part of the healing process.

I've begun to challenge the negative self-talk and limiting beliefs that once held me captive. When I find myself engaging in self-criticism or doubting my worth, I pause and reframe these thoughts with compassion and understanding, replacing negative narratives with affirmations that celebrate my resilience, strength, and unique qualities.

Setting boundaries and prioritizing my well-being has become a crucial part of my journey. I've learned to say "no" to situations or people that drain my energy or compromise my emotional health. I make self-care a non-negotiable part of my daily routine, engaging in activities that bring me joy, peace, and relaxation.

Cultivating a practice of self-discovery has been essential in reconnecting with my authentic self. I engage in activities like journaling, meditation, maintaining a vision board, pursuing my passions, exploring my values, beliefs, and dreams, and using this knowledge to guide my decisions and actions.

I've embraced the power of choice, recognizing that I have the agency to make decisions that align with my well-being and goals. I'm free to explore and form peaceful relationships based on honest foundations and not illusions. I trust my intuition and have faith in my ability to create a life that reflects my deepest desires and values.

Celebrating my progress and practicing gratitude has become a daily ritual. I acknowledge the milestones, both big and small, that mark my journey of self-discovery and healing. I regularly express gratitude for the lessons, experiences, and people that have shaped my path and contributed to my growth.

A remarkable shift occurred on January 1, 2024, when I awoke with an all-encompassing sense of joy, purpose, and unbridled optimism for the future. It was as if the burdens of my past had been lifted, allowing me to breathe deeply and freely for the first time in years. This profound happiness was rooted in the realization that I possessed the power to shape my life according to my deepest desires, unencumbered by the chains of trauma and pain that had once held me captive.

To you, dear reader, I offer this message from the depths of my heart: You are not alone in your struggles, and your past does not define your future. Your story, like mine, is one of resilience, courage, and the indomitable human spirit. Embrace the transformative power of self-love and forgiveness, for it is through these profound acts that we heal, grow, and become the architects of our own destinies.

Every step you take towards self-discovery and healing is a testament to your strength and the boundless potential that resides within you. Trust in the journey, even when the path seems uncertain, for it is in the crucible of adversity that we forge the most beautiful versions of ourselves. Let your faith be your guiding light, illuminating the way forward and reminding you of the extraordinary purpose that awaits you.

No lie, I "woke up happy" on January 1, 2024, and have been doing so every day since then. I make the conscious decision daily to live an intentional life full of joy and hope in what God has in store for ME. I am the master of my own destiny, courageously navigating the depths of my soul with unwavering self-trust. With each step, I ignite the beacons of belief, illuminating my path toward a life of boundless love, artful success, and joyful peace.

I am the navigator of my own journey, and with each breath, I affirm my commitment to thrive in the soft life I envision for myself. I stand at the bow of my ship, the wind of change caressing my face, and I know that I am exactly where I am meant to be. The journey has been long, the battles hard-fought, but every step has led me to this moment of profound understanding.

As I set forth on this new voyage, I carry with me the lessons of my past, the wisdom of my present, and the boundless hope of my future. I am a woman reborn, a phoenix rising from the ashes of her former life, ready to embrace the extraordinary journey that awaits. The symphony of the sea echoes my inner harmony, and with the heralding call of the gulls, I step into the next chapter of my existence, where the whispers of the past become the foundation of my tomorrow, and the dance of life continues, ever graceful, ever resilient.

About Melissa Andrewin

Melissa is a Southern California native, through and through, and she loves it there! Her career background is in construction project management, and she is currently employed at a large community college. She holds a Bachelor's Degree in Public Administration from the University of La Verne. One of her long-term personal goals is to obtain her certification to teach construction safety inspections.

She is also very active in her District's union, serving the member base by reconciling employee-management relations challenges and advocating for healthy work environments campus-wide. Her most prized achievement and accomplishment to date is embracing her past experiences and leaning into who she really is, outside of who the world and others have told her she is.

After enduring many tumultuous relationships and events, she has developed an empathic spirit and accepted her gift to connect and be a listening ear to hurting souls. She has two adult daughters who are her most favorite people in the world.

She enjoys a broad range of self-care activities such as gardening (though plants scream at her not to buy them!), cooking, exploring new places and meeting new people, interior decorating, natural hair/skin/nail care, and staying active (walking, cycling, dancing, gym workouts, jumping off cliffs into the waters of Jamaica, etc., as long as her life is not at risk). She especially enjoys live musical events, comedy shows, museums, and almost anything surrounding Black culture, including visual and performing arts, literature, and more.

Connect with Melissa

IG: @melisifent

CHAPTER 7

THE ART OF MINDFUL REBUILDING: PRACTICES FOR HEALING THE MIND, BODY, AND SPIRIT AFTER TRAUMA

Roberta Bell

Harness the mindful mastery of presence, forgiveness, and balance to fortify your essence, cultivating strength and empathy for an empowered future.

The story begins within the depths of the soul, where vulnerability and strength intertwine. We meet you, the reader, embarking on a journey of self-reclamation. This is not just about mending past wounds, but about weaving a "Tapestry of Transformation," one that merges your essence with the strength of a brighter future.

Imagine a tapestry – each thread a lesson learned, a victory won, a moment of clarity amidst life's relentless waves. These threads represent wisdom gleaned from pain, the scars that map a warrior's journey. Every thread woven strengthens your tapestry, an emblem of resilience, unwavering spirit, and enduring grace.

This chapter is where we begin the alchemical process of transforming sorrow into wisdom. We learn to craft our tapestry with intention and unwavering resolve, to paint its warp and weft with the vibrant colors of our deepest desires and aspirations.

Guiding you are the "Pillars of Presence" – structures grounded in the profound art of mindfulness. Through presence, you discover the secrets of living fully within each breath, each heartbeat, and each fleeting moment. This foundation allows you to weave the present moment into the very fabric of your being.

In the artful reclamation of self, the pillars of presence stand vigilant, a testament to the fortitude of the human spirit and the transformative power of mindfulness. Their foundation is strong, built with mindful practices that restore the soul and mend the fabric of our very being. The art of mindful rebuilding is not a singular act, but a mosaic of efforts, each stone a practice that guides us to the tranquility of healing.

Embarking on this path requires an open heart, the kind that beats with the courage to face what is—and the grace to accept it. This courage becomes the chisel with which we sculpt away the veneer of pain, revealing the glistening core of our true essence. It is in these moments of lucid presence that our spirit reconnects with the vibrancy of life, each breath a stroke of the artist's brush on the canvas of our universe.

Imagine for a moment the tender touch of awareness on the rough edges of our inner turmoil. Like the gentle hands of a healer, our conscious mind tends to the wounds of our memory, applying the salve of attentiveness with delicate precision. As we nurture ourselves with this care, the echoes of past traumas grow fainter, their grip loosening, allowing the light of introspection and compassion to pour in.

Guided by the Pillars of Presence, we engage in practices that steady our core. Meditation becomes our sacred ritual, a daily convening with silence that speaks volumes. Journaling, a sacred scribe of the soul's journey, captures the outpourings of our innermost thoughts, providing a mirror into the depths of who we are. Yoga, that ancient dance of body and breath, intertwines our physical form with the pulse of life, rendering us supple and strong, ready to bend with the winds of fate without breaking.

From awareness emerges the "Framework of Forgiveness," a structure whose strength lies not in rigidity but in letting go. Here, you'll delicately chisel away the shackles that inhibit your heart's full blossoming, carving a space for light and love to reside, summoning your limitless potential.

The tapestry doesn't shy away from storms; it gathers its luminescence from every challenge. Within the "Sanctuary of Strength," you will discover the tenacity to endure, to emerge from the storm stronger, more resilient, and fueled by the inner fire of empowerment.

As we navigate this framework, remember the Pillars of Presence our hearts have laid brick by sturdy brick. We move with attention and intention, acknowledging each hurt, each aching memory, as real and valid—and then, with the same breath that gives voice to our pain, we expel it and set our spirit free. With every act of forgiveness, we give ourselves permission to heal, step away from the ties that have bound us to what was, and step into the boundless potential of what lies ahead.

Forgiveness is an artistry—one that colors our world with hues of understanding and shades of grace. It does not ask us to forget the trials or gloss over the depth of our trials; rather, it requires the strength to accept them and the courage to transcend them. It is a sculptor's touch, tender yet transformative, reshaping the heart into a vessel not just for survival, but for thriving.

To stand in the midst of stormy recollections, to weather the gales of regret with the steadiness of a mountain—that is our course of action. Here, the pen of personal narrative rewrites the stories that once held us captive. In place of the crumpled pages filled with despair, we etch new chapters where the protagonists—ourselves—embrace growth and dance with hope.

Every scribe knows the power of the written word—the ink that seeped into the fabric of the parchment never truly fades. Yet, it is the empowered author who grasps the quill firmly, composing fresh prose upon the old text. We become cartographers of the heart, redrawing boundaries with lines that curve towards empathy, extending the latitude of our understanding, and broadening the longitude of our compassion.

We must recognize the dual nature of this task. The practice of forgiving others intertwines with the equally significant journey of self-forgiveness. The two are the warp and weft of the same cloth, each reinforcing the other, strengthening the weave of our resilience. It is in the quiet acknowledgment of our own faults and missteps that we find the truest path to self-compassion and growth..

Empathy is the golden thread that heals and connects. It binds us together in a symphony of shared experiences, reminding you that you are not alone.

Within these walls, we cultivate a strength that speaks softly yet carries an indelible mark of authority. It is a mantle that rests on the shoulders of those who have learned the intricate balance between yielding and asserting—a harmony achieved not in solitude but in the melody of shared humanity.

As we fortify our internal fortress, we recognize that the true measure of might is found in the fertility of our compassion, the integrity of our resolve, and the unassailable power of our unity. Here, in this garden of grit, we kneel to touch the earth, our hands cupped to sow the seeds of empowerment that blossom into flowers of action, their fragrance a testament to our transformative journey.

And now, with the resilience of our sanctuary interwoven with the tenacity of our spirit, we glance towards the echoes that resound beyond these walls. An orchestra of empathy awaits us, ready to harmonize with the resonance of our own pulsating strength. As we step forward, our resolve echoes the cadences of the past, each stride a note in the symphony of our narrative—the opus of empowerment now ready to embrace the symphony of shared experiences, rich with the undertones of understanding and the promise of a collective tomorrow.

The mindful rebuilding of self is a mosaic of practices, each piece a guidepost on the path to healing. Embarking on this path requires an open heart, one that embraces what is with courage and accepts it with grace.

Imagine the gentle touch of awareness on the raw edges of your turmoil. Like a healer's hands, your conscious mind tends to the wounds of your memory, applying the salve of attentiveness with delicate precision. As you nurture yourself, the echoes of past traumas fade, allowing light and introspection to pour in.

Practices like meditation, journaling, and yoga become your sacred rituals. Meditation is your daily communion with silence, a space where volumes are spoken without a word. Journaling becomes a confidante, capturing the outpourings of your innermost thoughts, revealing the depths of who you are. Yoga, the ancient dance of body and breath, strengthens and aligns you, preparing you to bend with life's winds without breaking.

As you cultivate these practices, you become the gardener of your mind. Seeds of awareness require time to root and bloom, transforming the landscape of your inner world. Remember, mighty trees were once fragile saplings.

The journey of healing often involves navigating the murky waters of self-forgiveness. It's easy to get stuck replaying past mistakes, the weight of guilt a heavy anchor on the soul. But self-forgiveness isn't about condoning past actions. It's about acknowledging your humanity, and the choices you made with the knowledge you had at the time. It's about releasing the burden of self-blame and extending the same compassion you might offer a friend to yourself. This act of self-love creates space for growth, allowing you to learn from the past without being chained to it.

With self-forgiveness, a lightness arises. The crippling grip of shame loosens, replaced by a newfound sense of self-acceptance. You can begin to see yourself not as a collection of past mistakes, but as a work in progress, capable of learning and evolving. This newfound freedom fuels your journey of healing, allowing you to move forward with a lighter heart and a brighter future.

Within this garden of renewal, forgiveness is the fertile soil. By pulling the weeds of resentment, you make way for new growth. Forgiveness is not just for others, but for yourself. We all unknowingly build barriers around our hearts. The freedom found in forgiveness clears the skies for empathy to shine through.

Your tapestry is not woven alone. The robust fabric is strengthened by the threads of community. Connection fuels your rebuilding with shared strength and collective wisdom. In the "Sanctuary of Strength," surrounded by those who resonate with your struggle, true healing flourishes. Here, a chorus of voices sings the anthem of recovery, leading you gently to the next phase – the fertile ground of forgiveness.

The practice of meditation coalesces with the symphony of self-care, nurturing the roots of the sanctified tree within us. Our meditations share a kinship with the rich earth that cradles them, allowing stillness to permeate our being, granting us the sapience to divest from the superfluous and invest in the substantive. The very act of breathing in sync with the cosmos instills a reverence for the manifold elements that comprise our days—our work, our passions, our relationships, and our dreams—all demanding a wise adjudication of our time and spirit.

In the orchestration of our commitments, we compose a melody that sings of both ambition and peace. We harness the fervency of our aspirations, the flame that flickers with the desire to make our mark upon the world, while also embracing the quietude that whispers of self-compassion and healing reprieve. Striking a balance is not the silencing of either voice but the harmonious integration that allows each its vibrant expression in the concert of our lives.

This crafted balance is not a static construct but a living, breathing tapestry that adjusts to the winds of change and the evolution of our journey. It invites us to continually assess and realign our priorities, ensuring they still resonate with the core of who we have become and who we are yet to be. This meticulous calibration of life's engine ensures that our voyage sails smoothly along the intended course, buoyed by the depths of self-knowing and the heights of purposeful action.

With the architecture of equilibrium in place, the blueprint for balance now an indelible part of our repertoire, we stand poised at the cusp of valorous revelation. Having mastered the pulse of presence and the harmony of healing, we are ready to journey forth, carrying our blueprint as a compass, directing us toward the fertile lands of new opportunities and the dawn of renewed strength. Ahead lies the vision of valor, a beckoning field of possibility where the seeds of our resilience and wisdom are sown, promising a harvest rich with the fruits of enduring empowerment.

The "Framework of Forgiveness" is like dawn's light, dispelling the lingering darkness of the past. It is a conscious unburdening, a liberation of the soul from the weight of past grievances and self-blame.

As you move through this framework, acknowledge each hurt and aching memory as real and valid. Then, with the same breath, you release it and set your spirit free. Each act of forgiveness allows you to heal, step away from the past, and embrace the boundless potential of what lies ahead.

Forgiveness is an art – one that colors your world with understanding.

About Roberta Bell

Roberta Bell, Roberta The Tool Lady, is a multifaceted individual who empowers others through her work as a podcaster, therapist, writer, and life coach. She uses her diverse skillset and passion to provide practical tools and support for mental well-being, personal growth, and achieving life goals. Her reach extends beyond individual sessions through her podcast and online presence, making her a valuable resource for many. Specializing in "I Think Myself Happy!"

Connect with Roberta

IG: @robertathetoollady

FB: @live.l.williams

TT: @robertathetoollady

YT: @roberta_thetoollady

CHAPTER 8

HER LIFE REWRITTEN: CRAFTING YOUR COMEBACK STORY WITH COURAGE
Nannette Palmore

In the furnace of adversity, fan your embers of valor, forging a triumphant destiny from the trials that seek to temper you.

Growing up in the projects was tough. My grandma, aka Ma, raised me with lots of love, but there were still so many hard things I had to face. When I was little, I felt like having a male figure would fill the void of not having a father. I had my uncles and a great-uncle, and they were amazing, but a young girl without an actual father still wanted one. But that wasn't the case. The stepfather I ended up with became the worst enemy a child or woman could ever have. I became a victim of sexual abuse and rape at a very early age. After slowly overcoming some of that, receiving justice, and seeing this man go to prison, I would later encounter the exact same thing. I thought I was past it, but then the unthinkable happened - I was raped again at 15 by a popular guy in the neighborhood. No one would've believed me if I told, because I was trying to fit in, inviting people over on nights my grandma was away and trying to get them out before Ma came home. It happened in the privacy of my own home. That individual was later shot and killed. It was like God was saying, "I saw what happened." Once again, I felt helpless and alone.

As a child, I often felt like God didn't exist in my life, even though I was in church several nights a week. Why didn't anyone help me? Why didn't anybody see what I was going through? But after that second time, I started to believe somebody did see, someone did understand. I always looked up because I always went to church and looked on my wall at a plaque Ma gave me that was the serenity prayer. I started thinking about a way out.

Sometimes it felt like God wasn't there for me, like no one saw the pain I was going through. But deep down, I knew someone was watching over me. I had to find my own way out. College wasn't an option without money, and almost straight A's and B's, yet failing or below average in a class here or there that was majorly important, so I joined the Army. It gave me the discipline and strength I needed to keep pushing forward. I wanted to be a professional choreographer, but Ma said it wasn't a real job. So the Army became my way out of the hood. I never wanted it to be my life, just out of a town where I had so many memories of hurt, pain, and mischief.

Shortly after I had already signed up for the Army, I met a familiar man who I thought was my soulmate. We got married and had two awesome sons. People would call us Bonnie and Clyde because we seemed inseparable. But then slowly the drugs and the abuse started. I never saw it coming. We both came from the same make-it-or-break-it town and thought we understood each other, as we were a classic opposites attract couple. But slowly our lifestyle changed, employment obstacles hit, and old ways amongst us both took over. There were probably generational curses on both sides. I thought we interacted well, and that we meshed, but really, our differences, sense of humor, love for family, and popularity made us cling to each other in what would end in an unhealthy way.

I often chose to separate myself from certain situations as if these things wouldn't happen to me. That's how I saw the first situation. He'll never hit me, even though I heard he hit others. He'll never hurt me, even though I heard he hurt others. He'll never distance himself from his sons, etc. This was a pattern of behavior.

I had to get out to protect myself and my boys. With the help of a domestic violence shelter, I fled North Carolina, my home, leaving all my family behind. I arrived in Georgia with nothing but my kids, all their belongings that fit, and the 1 outfit I had on. We were homeless, sleeping in sketchy hotels, not knowing if we'd make it. One hotel had an actual pimp knocking on my door half the night, thinking I was the prostitute who owed him money. My oldest son would tell me after he was grown that he thought it was a nightmare, but it was real. I had to protect my sons. I kept praying because I knew I had to make a better life for us.

On the 3rd morning, I called 211 United Way and finally got Partnership Against Domestic Violence. They housed me and my kids for about three months before I had to find my own placement. I met another man who I thought would be my protector, but he had his own demons. I ignored the red flags because I felt obligated to him for helping me. I stayed a few months until I won money on a scratch-off ticket. That was my ticket out, God showing me a way. But the pattern repeated. I met a man during my "rebound era" who seemed nice, and who helped me when I was stranded. But I overlooked the signs again.

Please don't think I'm blaming one person for any issue. At the end of the day, you have to take a step back and look at yourself, what it is that you attract, and also what you bring to a situation. I could not figure out at that time what it was that I kept doing that was putting me in these situations until relationship number 3, the guy I thought would be, "the 1." After the most heartbreaking breakup from him, who my sons adored, I stopped.

I had to love myself first. I spent almost five years single, before realizing my worth. I did a lot of ratchet stuff and lived a pretty wild life. But near the end of that time, I was tired. I was ready to settle down, but now I was emotionally attached to people who never were gonna make me theirs because I had to love myself. I kept attracting the same kind of pain because I hadn't healed. Once I regained my self-worth, I became ok with being single. I started detaching from people. I had to learn that I kept attracting the same type of man because I hadn't healed my childhood traumas. I was used to a certain type, groomed to be attracted to what was familiar, even if it was toxic.

Looking back, I see that every obstacle was a chance for me to rise up. The sexual abuse, the domestic violence, the homelessness, losing everything in an apartment fire, and having to start over - it all taught me how resilient I am. I had to learn to face my pain instead of running from it. I had to learn that my past doesn't define me. With every challenge, I grew a little taller. Now I stand as a business owner, with my own catering company. Corporate America counted me out and I bet on myself. The same day they started outsourcing jobs, I got my business license. The same day I got let go, I set my new life plan in motion. God had a plan.

Sometimes in life as women, we're just moving too fast. We're so busy working the hours and jobs to pay the bills and getting all the things that our children need that we fail to see certain things that are right in front of our faces. It's not an excuse. It's called accountability. You have to be accountable for your actions when you start working on yourself.

My journey hasn't been pretty. I've made mistakes and had my heart broken more times than I can count, subjected myself to things with men and women that I don't regret, but definitely could've done without. But

I've also found my strength, my faith, and my purpose. I'm not just a survivor, I'm a warrior. I'm a mother of two amazing sons, a grandmother, a wife, an entrepreneur, and now an author. I turned my trials into triumph, my pain into power. I had to take responsibility for my part in the patterns. I had to dig deep and figure out why I kept involving myself in the same kind of chaos. It wasn't easy facing those truths, but it set me free.

To every woman who's reading this, I want you to know that you're not alone. Your story may have some dark chapters, but it's not over yet. You have the power to rewrite your ending. It won't be easy, but it will be worth it.

You are not damaged goods. You are not your worst mistake. You are a force of nature, a queen, a survivor. Your scars are not shameful, they are sacred. They are reminders of what you've overcome. Wear them with pride.

Give yourself time to heal. Be patient with your progress. Surround yourself with people who lift you up, not tear you down. Set boundaries and stick to them. Sometimes that means leaving your whole life behind to protect yourself and your peace. It means choosing yourself even when it's scary.

Remember, your kids are watching you. They're learning from your example. Show them what it means to be brave, to fight for a better life, and sacrifices, and to never give up. Break the cycles that held you back so they can fly free. My sons saw me struggle, but they also saw me rise. Now they know what a strong woman looks like. My prayer has always been that they not only respect me but other women as well.

Most of all, fall in love with yourself. Treat yourself with the kindness and respect you deserve. Celebrate your wins, big and small. Whether it's becoming a mom at an early age, being in multiple abuse situations, moving from a shelter, getting settled, or starting a business, forgive yourself. No more beating yourself up, sis. You're doing the best you can with what you've got.

I won't lie and say it's going to be all sunshine. Life will keep throwing curveballs. You'll have days where you want to quit. But keep showing up for yourself. Keep believing in your dreams. Even when you lose everything. You have the strength inside you to rebuild.

The woman you see now is Nannette Palmore, a.k.a. China, owner of MealsbyChina LLC. I am a mother, a grandmother, a wife, an entrepreneur, a concession trailer owner, and now, an author. I'm rewriting my story and helping other women do the same.

One day, you're going to look back on this season and be so damn proud of how far you've come. You're going to see how every scar, every heartache, every setback was shaping you into the woman you were meant to be. You're going to realize that you had the strength inside you all along.

Your comeback is coming, and it's going to be glorious. And when you doubt yourself, just remember: if Nannette can do it, so can you. We're in this together. Our stories are still being written, and the best is yet to come.

About Nannette Palmore

Nannette Palmore, affectionately known as China, grew up in Lumberton, NC, under the loving care of her grandmother, Queen Wright. From an early age, she found joy and solace in helping her grandmother cook for prominent business families. Despite facing numerous childhood adversities, cooking became her source of peace and joy.

In 1997, at 20, Nannette joined the US Army to support herself, escape project living, and fund her education. She married her childhood crush in 1998 and was honorably discharged in 2000 due to medical conditions. Returning to their hometown with their first son, the family soon grew with the birth of their second son, Xavier. Nannette worked in retail, management, and as a Loan Adjuster at BBT bank until 2004 when an unexpected separation led her and her sons to Atlanta, GA.

In Atlanta, Nannette juggled multiple roles, including retail management, nursing assistant, and a part-time licensed stylist. Her passion for cooking flourished, gaining her a following through corporate events and promotional groups. In 2017, amid corporate job cuts, she took a leap of faith and founded MealsByChina, LLC, offering catering, meal preps, and pan dishes to go. Although she started chef school at Le Cordon Bleu, she couldn't complete it, but she earned certifications in food safety and sanitation, enhancing her culinary skills.

When her corporate job was finally cut, Nannette felt a profound sense of freedom. She embraced her passion fully, promising to deliver "An angelic dining experience." Her journey continues, driven by her love for cooking and her resilience in the face of life's challenges.

Connect with Nannette

IG: @MealsbyChinallc

FB: @MealsByChinaLLC

CHAPTER 9

FROM NOTHING TO SOMETHING: A TRUE STORY OF GOD'S REDEMPTION

Samantha Dantzler

Unfaltering perseverance paves the path upward, fueled by faith, nurtured by wisdom, each stride a testament to personal power and self-worth.

As the looming peak of my destiny called to me, beckoning me to test my resolve, I stood at the base camp of transformation, a sacred space to prepare for the ascent towards self-worth and personal power. Here, in the stillness before the climb, I grounded myself, taking inventory of my strength and the path trodden thus far.

With the echoes of past victories whispering in my soul, I readied myself for the climb. My eyes fixed on the heights where my fullest potential awaited, unshackled by fear's grasp and buoyed by the winds of change. I knew the journey ahead would test me, but I was determined to rise.

You see, I've always been a trusting person, sometimes to a fault. That trust has led me down paths of heartache and pain, none more so than the 27-year road of addiction that nearly claimed my life. It's funny how friendships can start out so sweet, wrapped in the promise of connection and support. But not all friends are true, and some are merely foes in disguise, sent to steal, kill, and destroy.

I remember the first time I tried cocaine. It was at a party, and I was young and naive. The rush was unlike anything I'd ever experienced, and I felt invincible. Little did I know that this feeling would become my downfall, the siren song that lured me into the depths of addiction.

By the grace of God, I survived. And though the scars of my past remain, they serve as reminders of the battles I've won and the strength I possess. Now, 12 years clean, I stand at the base of a new mountain, ready to climb toward the life I know I deserve.

The initial steps of my ascent were a pact between me and my heart's steadfast tenacity. I found my footing amidst the rubble of life's trek - the scars of abuse, the quicksand of addiction, the shattered pieces of my once fractured self.

I thought of my mother, lost to the very same demons I fought. Her death, a bitter pill to swallow, became a catalyst for change. I couldn't let her story end in vain. I had to break the cycle, if not for myself, then for the generations to come.

I remember the day I found out about my mother's passing. It was a hot shot, they said - a lethal mixture of heroin and cocaine. The news hit me like a freight train, and I crumbled under the weight of grief and guilt. I was a mother myself, and yet here I was, following in her footsteps, dancing with death.

The trail to clarity was carved with the steppingstones of hard-won lessons and the muscular resolve bestowed by endurance. I laid down strategies for maintaining a rhythmic stride that respected my pace while championing my persistence in the face of every upward challenge. Each step, though heavy at times, propelled me forward.

Success on the peaks is as much about the breath as the step. As I climbed, I focused on the breath of belief - those essential inhalations that oxygenated my spirit with hope and vitality.

I thought of my children, the beacons of light in my darkest nights. They were the reason I fought, the reason I couldn't give up. Every breath I took was for them, a promise to be the mother they deserved.

I remember the day my first grandchild was born. As I held her in my arms, I felt a love so fierce, so protective, that it shook me to my core. I knew then that I had to change, that I couldn't let this precious child see me as a shadow of myself, lost in the haze of addiction.

I took deep, intentional breaths of faith that infused my ascent with the fresh air of inspiration. Breathing became a sacred rhythm, syncing my internal strength to the external challenges. Moment after moment, I climbed toward epic vistas of self-actualization, my lungs expanding with the conviction that I was capable of conquering the mountain within.

With every heart-pumping stretch, there were plateaus - moments that beckoned complacency, whispering seductively for me to settle. But I was dedicated to propelling myself beyond the flatlands of satisfaction. I had to fuel my thirst to continue progressing, even when the summit winked from the farthest clouds.

I remembered the countless times I had fallen, the relapses that had nearly broken me. But each time, I rose again, dusted myself off, and kept climbing. I couldn't let the plateaus of momentary comfort lull me into stagnation.

I remember the day I celebrated my first year of sobriety. It was a small victory, but it felt like a mountain moved. I had fought tooth and nail for that milestone, and I wasn't about to let it slip away. I knew that complacency was the enemy of progress, and I had to keep pushing and keep climbing.

I harnessed the warmth of persistence to maintain momentum. With techniques to keep me steadfast, I ensured that my journey's pace was marked by an unwavering commitment to the soaring heights of success I sought. I would not rest until I reached the peak.

In the solace of altitude, as I ascended, the winds of wisdom carried messages, ancient whispers that eddied around the crags of life's complex cliffside. With every step upward, I tuned into these murmurs, allowing them to enfold me in the fables and folklore of those who had climbed before me.

I sought solace in the stories of others who had overcome, in the pages of books that mirrored my struggle. I found mentors in unexpected places, wise souls who had weathered their own storms and emerged victorious. Their whispers became my guideposts, their triumphs my inspiration.

I remember the day I met my sponsor, a woman who had walked the path of recovery long before I had even taken my first step. Her strength, her resilience, her unwavering faith in the power of transformation - they became my anchor, my North Star in the darkest of nights.

I learned to navigate my path with the compass of enlightened insight, relying on the gales of guidance as welcome companions in my ascent. Their gentle nudges steered me clear of treacherous terrain and illuminated hidden footholds of opportunity. In their whispers, I found the courage to climb on.

The higher I climbed, the further I could see. As I approached the summit, a panoramic view unfurled before me, immersing me in a scenic overlook where horizons of potential stretched out infinitely.

I saw a future where my children could be proud of their mother, where the chains of generational trauma were broken. I saw a life of purpose and passion, where my story could become a beacon of hope for others lost in the depths of their own struggles.

I remember the day I started my first business. It was a small venture, but it was mine - a testament to the power of second chances, of rising from the ashes of a life once lost. I poured my heart and soul into that business, knowing that every success, no matter how small, was a step toward the future I had envisioned.

Through reflective exercises and vision-casting, I gained the vantage point to chart my continued ascent. Strategic milestones marked each progress point like beacons of achievement, providing encouragement and direction as I scaled my way toward the crowning summit of my journey. From this elevated perspective, anything seemed possible.

As daybreak crowned the mountaintop, I embraced the summit of selfhood. Here, in the solstice of success, I stood triumphant, bathed in the first light of dawn - the symbolic rise into the day of self-realization.

I thought of all the versions of myself I had shed along the way - the addict, the victim, the broken shell of a woman. I had climbed through the sorrow, the shame, and the shadows of my past to emerge here, at the pinnacle of my becoming.

I remember the day I looked in the mirror and saw not a stranger, but a survivor. A warrior. A woman who had fought her way back from the brink of destruction and emerged victorious. I saw a reflection of resilience, of strength, of unbreakable spirit.

An affirmation welled up from my own conquering spirit: "I am a mountain of strength, unshakable in my resolve to claim the life of purpose and joy that I deserve. With each step, I rise above my past and ascend to new heights of self-discovery and love. I am the author of my own redemption, the heroine of my own tale. I stand tall in the face of adversity, rooted in the knowledge that I am worthy, I am powerful, I am free. No longer will I be shackled by the chains of addiction, for I have found liberation in the light of recovery. I am a living testament to the power of transformation, a beacon of hope for all those still struggling in the darkness. I am unbreakable, unshakable, unstoppable. I am the embodiment of resilience, the epitome of strength, the champion of my own destiny. And with each breath, each step, each triumph, I rise ever higher, ever closer to the woman I was always meant to be."

I basked in the glow of this hard-won victory, knowing that though the landscape of my life would continue to undulate with valleys and peaks, I now possessed the tools, tenacity, and triumphal spirit to navigate whatever lay ahead. For in the end, it is not the mountain we conquer, but ourselves.

About Samantha Dantzler

Samantha was born in Brooklyn New York; she is the 5th child to her parents Fred and Carol. After the death of her mother, she went into the care of family, friends, and the foster care system. After overcoming life's challenges and obstacles she went on to have 3 children and 7 grandchildren. She now owns 3 businesses and lives in Georgia.

Connect with Samantha

IG: @SamanthaDantzler

CHAPTER 10

THE CHAMELEON'S QUEST: RISING ABOVE THE LABELS TO LIVE YOUR TRUTH

Tamara Sidney

The melody of your mind needs the harmony of your heart to birth wisdom's eloquent symphony.

My earliest memory is of the crisp spring air in Lexington, Kentucky in 1979. Even at just five years old, my mind pulsed with intelligence and awareness far beyond my tender age. There was an insatiable curiosity within me, a drive to explore and understand the world around me. This thirst for knowledge was nurtured by my father, who had an unwavering belief in my abilities. He would encourage me to tackle each new day as an opportunity to learn, grow, and conquer my limitations.

The sacred ritual of Saturday mornings is forever etched into my soul. I can still smell the tantalizing aroma of pancake batter sizzling as my father rose early to prepare those delectable discs. It was more than just breakfast – it was a special bond between us, a dance of love and trust. With each movement, and each shared smile, my father imparted the profound belief that I could accomplish anything I set my mind to. Those pancake lessons were the foundation for the unshakeable confidence that burned within my young spirit.

On one such morning, a spark ignited that would change the course of my life forever. I had watched intently, absorbing every nuance as my father worked his culinary sorcery. And on this day, I knew it was my turn to create the magic. A surprise for my parents – a breakfast lovingly crafted by my own tiny hands to fill them with pride and joy.

The sizzling aroma wafting from the pancakes was a siren's call, beckoning my mother with the promise of an indulgent morning delight. But instead of the praise I had envisioned, my innocent efforts were met with scolding words that pierced my belief in myself like icy needles. As my mother stumbled in with eyes still heavy from slumber, the blissful dream of creating such a special surprise for my parents shattered into shards of disbelief and hurt.

In that pivotal moment burned into my memory forever, something dark and cruel manifested in my mother. Consumed by frustration at the perceived transgression of a child daring to take responsibility, she committed an act so brutal, so devastating, that the wounds have never fully healed. With an anger that still haunts me, she pressed my small left hand onto the scorching red-hot eye of the electric stove. White-hot pain lanced through me as the searing heat seared my flesh down to the bone.

My anguished screams filled the kitchen as the throbbing agony of the burn seared my body and soul. The tantalizing aroma of pancakes was overwhelmed by the acrid, sickening stench of singed skin – a miasma that threatened to make me retch. Rational thoughts fled in the wake of this primitive torment, this betrayal committed by the person I looked to for love and protection.

In vain, my mother shouted justifications meant to explain her cruelty. How could such flimsy words ever penetrate the maelstrom of shock, pain, and confusion raging inside me? In that moment of crisis, my world and everything I had believed in lay in smoldering ruins around me. The unwavering belief instilled by my father that I could conquer any challenge? Gone, incinerated by the searing hatred in my mother's actions. Her act spoke louder than any empty reassurances – she did not believe in me, in my capabilities. That cold, devastating rejection cut deeper than any physical wound ever could.

A part of me died that day and went into permanent hiding. I resolved from the depths of my shattered psyche to never again reveal my skills to my mother, to never use my left hand in her presence. For in her twisted mind, left-handedness carried the taint of evil, of something sinister and unholy. In my fragile innocence, I believed I must have invited this torment upon myself by committing the transgression of pursuing greatness. The very act of creation – the simple joy of crafting a special breakfast – had rendered me a servant of the devil in her eyes.

The pancake incident carved deep, indelible scars not just upon my hand, but into the very fabric of my identity and self-worth. My self-esteem and self-assurance lay in shattered ruins around me. With devastating clarity, I realized that my own mother – the person who should have nurtured and cherished my precocious spirit – could never understand or appreciate my uniqueness. The gifts that should have been celebrated became Instead sources of cruel rejection and torment.

Yet from the scorched ashes of that defining childhood trauma, a resilient fire ignited within the very core of my being. A blaze of determination to rise up and advocate for myself and others facing such injustice. To stand firm in defending the right to embrace one's unique identity without shame or subjugation. To believe in myself no matter how harsh the circumstances or how brutal the opposition. This became my unshakeable bedrock of survival.

As I grew, that brilliant inner flame allowed my intuitive, genius-minded nature to blossom like a resilient desert flower pushing upwards through the cracked, dry earth. I learned to trust my instincts and let my innate intelligence be the compass that would guide me through all of life's challenges and darkness. Over the ensuing years, I became renowned for my uncanny ability to transcend conventional thinking and illuminate solutions that existed outside the limited silo of societal boundaries.

This awakening catalyzed an unquenchable thirst for knowledge that propelled me to devour books and insights from every conceivable source. I was an insatiable learner, an explorer without limits, driven to expand my understanding of the human spirit and condition. My singular gifts of intuition and penetrating vision, intertwined with an unwavering devotion to walking my own authentic path, ultimately revealed my true calling - to transform my personal quest for understanding into a beacon of healing for countless others struggling to express their highest human potential.

When I reflect upon that traumatic pancake incident, I know it was a crucible that forever forged my identity and deepest values. It was a pivotal moment that tested the tensile strength of my resilience and emerged having galvanized my resolve to never allow anyone or any circumstance to diminish the brilliant light of my uniqueness. The scars will endure, but they also stand as reminders that true self-acceptance must be cultivated from within - that believing in yourself is the key to overcoming any obstacle, no matter how daunting.

The voices of disbelief came first from the person who should have championed me above all others - my own mother. With an act of unconscionable viciousness etched permanently into my childhood memories, she shattered my innocent self-assurance into a kaleidoscope of anguish and self-doubt. She branded me as something twisted, something sinful and unholy, simply for possessing the audacity of a curious mind yearning to create and explore the world around me.

The weight of my mother's actions sits heavy on my heart, a burden I carry with me every day. Her cruelty, that defining moment of pain and betrayal, left scars not just on my skin but deep within my soul. It was a betrayal of the deepest kind, a violation of the trust and love that should exist between a mother and child. In her eyes, I was not worthy of love or respect. I was a disappointment, a failure, a reminder of all the ways she believed I fell short.

But I refuse to let her define me. I refuse to let her actions dictate the course of my life. I am more than the sum of her judgments, more than the scars she left behind. I am a survivor, a warrior, a phoenix rising from the ashes.

Each day, I take a step forward, reclaiming my power and my identity. I embrace my uniqueness, my creativity, and my intelligence. I refuse to hide in the shadows, to shrink myself down to fit into the boxes others try to place me in. I am bold, I am fierce, I am unapologetically myself.

With each new lash of cruelty from my mother's lacerating tongue and crippling actions, those smoldering embers within were stoked hotter and became an inferno of unbreakable self-belief. While she pressed my tiny hand against the punishing heat of the stove's glowing red eye, branding my skin with the grotesque sigil of her own self-loathing and spiritual decay, she could never conceive of the unflinching inner fire she was forging within me.

Yet even as the searing sting of her hatred seared its way through my flesh and deep into my soul, a defiant spark flickered to life in my core. A resilient ember burned defiantly, fueled by the unshakable belief instilled in me by my father's loving guidance. He nurtured the intrinsic gifts that terrified my mother – the probing intelligence, the insatiable thirst for understanding, the unwillingness to accept boundaries or limitations. Where she sought to extinguish the brilliant flames of my potential, he fanned them with a steady stream of encouragement and faith in my abilities.

The journey to self-acceptance is not an easy one. There are days when the weight of her words threatens to drag me down, to extinguish the flame of hope and resilience within me. But I refuse to let her win. I refuse to let her darkness consume me.

Instead, I choose to rise. I choose to shine brightly, to illuminate the world with my brilliance and my strength. I am a beacon of hope, a testament to the power of resilience and self-belief.

I embrace each new day as a fresh start, a chance to rewrite the narrative of my life. I am not a victim of my past, but a survivor. I am not limited by the expectations of others but empowered by my own potential.

The judgmental whispers of others, the doubts and skepticism they cast my way, are nothing compared to the fire that burns within me. I am not defined by my age, abilities, or limitations. I am defined by my courage, my tenacity, and my unwavering belief in myself.

So let them whisper their doubts behind cupped hands, let their skeptical glares bore into me like cloudbursts of icy rain lashing against a mountainside. I remain unmoved, unshaken, for my foundation is rock-solid adamantine forged in the scorching crucible of life's harshest injustices and cruelest betrayals.

I define myself through the brilliant prism of my indomitable spirit – a radiant composite of resilience, fortitude, and an unbreakable sense of self-worth.

When disbelievers squint their judgmental eyes my way and curl their lips in disdainful sneers, they fail to perceive the brilliant, all-consuming blaze at my very core. If they could shrug off the shackles of their constrained perception and allow their vision to penetrate beyond the superficial layers, they would be blinded and driven back by the intensity of my wildfire faith in myself. Every fiber of my being resonates with an undeniable sense of purpose, of knowing that the gifts weighing down the fragile branches of my existence are destined for meteoric flowering in their own cosmic rhythm.

So let them whisper their frail misgivings and cast their tawdry taunts from the shadows. I will meet their apprehension with the radiant resolve of a supernova ascending toward the dazzling infinite.

Like a phoenix, I rise. I rise above the pain, above the doubt, above the darkness. I spread my wings and soar, a testament to the indomitable spirit that resides within us all.

Remember, you are not a static being, but a dynamic, ever-unfolding masterpiece. Celebrate the journey, for it is in the act of becoming that we truly live.

About Tamara Sidney

With a compassionate heart and a wealth of experience, I am a 48-year-old mother of two, though I tragically lost one child. I cherish my role as a grandmother to three delightful grandchildren. My educational background includes 66 hand-selected college courses, and also an Associate's Degree in Psychology while furthering my expertise with certifications in Mindfulness and Holistic Therapy. Professionally, I am a dedicated Mental Energy Therapist, helping individuals harness their inner strength and positivity. As a Motivational Speaker, I inspire audiences to overcome obstacles and embrace personal growth. Additionally, my specialization as a Trauma Specialist allows me to provide crucial support and guidance to those navigating difficult experiences. Balancing my time between the US and Jamaica, I draw inspiration from both cultures, enriching my approach to healing and wellness. My life's mission is to spread hope, healing, and resilience, guiding others on their journey to mental and emotional well-being.

Connect with Tamara

FB: @TamaraSidney

FB: @NurdyThugEntertainment

IG: @EyesaidIamTam

TT: @EyesaidIamTam

YT: @EyssaidIamTam

CHAPTER 11

BREAKING THE SILENCE: CONFRONTING THE SHADOWS OF ABUSE

Stephanie Walker

In unbinding silence, chart your course with the compass of voice, steered by the winds of worthiness towards the lighthouse of your truth.

In unbinding silence, I chart my course with the compass of voice, steered by the winds of worthiness towards the lighthouse of my truth.

As I embark on this voyage, I raise the anchor of silence that has weighed heavy on my soul, setting sail toward expressive freedom. My journey is a pilgrimage to the sacred space where voice becomes the compass through the uncharted waters of my personal narrative. I venture forth with a survivor's courage, seeking to find my voice and use it as a resonant force that advocates, transforms, and claims my rightful power.

From the tender age of four until fifteen, I bore the burden of sexual abuse in my South Carolina home. The very place that should have been my sanctuary became a prison of unspoken horrors. I endured years of violation, my innocence stripped away by those who should have protected me. The weight of the unspeakable pressed upon my young soul, stifling my voice and shrouding my world in a suffocating silence. The trauma etched itself deep into my being, a wound that would shape my journey for years to come.

At fifteen, I made the courageous decision to flee the supposed safety of home, desperately seeking refuge from the nightmare that had consumed my childhood. However, instead of finding solace, I was thrust into an uncaring system that branded me a troublemaker. The scars of my trauma went unacknowledged as I was tossed from place to place like a discarded object, my cries for help falling on deaf ears. The system, meant to protect and nurture, only served to deepen my wounds and reinforce the belief that my voice held no power. The loneliness and despair threatened to engulf me, but a flicker of resilience refused to be extinguished.

Determined to build a better life for myself, I sought refuge in the Job Corps at eighteen. It was a chance to start anew, learn a trade, and create a future untainted by the shadows of my past. Yet even in this supposed haven, predators lurked, ready to exploit my vulnerability. Once again, I found myself a target, violated by those who saw me as nothing more than an object for their twisted desires. The cycle of abuse continued, and I retreated further into the silence that had become my armor, afraid to speak my truth for fear of the consequences that might follow. The weight of shame and self-doubt threatened to crush my spirit, but a spark of hope refused to be snuffed out.

Despite the unrelenting darkness that seemed to follow me, I refused to let it extinguish my spirit. I sought solace in education, pouring myself into my studies as a means of escape and empowerment. I immersed myself in work, finding purpose and strength in my ability to contribute and create. Through it all, I turned to the arts, using creativity as a lifeline, a way to express the emotions that words could not capture. The act of creation became a balm for my wounded soul, a way to process the pain and begin the long journey toward healing.

Yet even as I fought to build a life of my own, the wounds inflicted by my family continued to fester. I felt like an outcast, the black sheep whose existence was only acknowledged when it served their interests. The weight of their rejection and the unresolved trauma left me feeling lost and alone, yearning for a sense of belonging and acceptance. The void left by their abandonment ached like a physical wound, a constant reminder of the love and support I had been denied.

With a heavy heart, I made the difficult decision to leave behind the familiar and set out for Georgia. It was a leap of faith, a chance to start over in a new place where the shadows of my past might not follow. In this new land, I found something I had never experienced before: true friendship. Surrounded by people who embraced me for who I was, I began to heal, slowly shedding the layers of shame and silence that had suffocated me for so long. The warmth of their acceptance felt like a balm to my battered soul, a glimmer of hope in a world that had long felt cold and unforgiving.

As the years passed, I discovered a profound sense of purpose in helping others. Drawing strength from my own struggles, I became a beacon of hope for those who had endured similar traumas. I listened with an open heart, offering support and understanding to those who had been silenced and marginalized. Through my work, I found a way to transform my pain into a source of empowerment, not only for myself but for countless others. The act of service became a way to reclaim my power, to transmute the darkness of my past into a light that could guide others toward healing.

Motherhood brought new joys and challenges into my life, and I embraced the role with the same fierce determination that had carried me through my darkest moments. I poured my love and compassion into my children, determined to break the cycle of abuse and create a home filled with safety, love, and understanding. The love I gave to my children became a testament to my own resilience, a promise that the wounds of the past would not define their future.

However, my unwavering commitment to supporting those in need would eventually lead me down a path filled with betrayal and injustice.

In a cruel twist of fate, I found myself locked away in a prison, a place that felt all too familiar, echoing the horrors of my childhood. Within those confining walls, I encountered yet another predator, a man who saw me as nothing more than a target for his heinous desires. The very system meant to protect and rehabilitate became my new nightmare, as I grappled with the darkness that threatened to consume me once more. The betrayal cut deep, a searing reminder of the injustices I had faced throughout my life.

But even in the midst of this unimaginable ordeal, my unbreakable spirit refused to be extinguished. I clung to the hope that had carried me through so many trials, determined to survive and emerge stronger than ever before. And in a moment of long-awaited justice, my abuser was finally held accountable for his crimes, bringing a glimmer of closure to the wounds that had haunted me for so long. The victory, hard-fought and long-overdue, felt like a vindication of my struggle, a testament to the power of my voice.

With newfound strength and an unsilenced voice, I made the courageous decision to share my story with the world. I refused to let shame or fear dictate my path any longer, embracing the power of my truth as a weapon against the darkness. Through my words, I found liberation, shattering the chains of silence that had once held me captive. My story became a beacon of hope for countless others, a testament to the resilience of the human spirit in the face of unimaginable adversity. The act of sharing my truth became a catalyst for healing, not only for myself but for all those who found solace in my words.

My odyssey to vocal resurgence was an intimate excavation, a tenacious unearthing of the articulate soul behind the barriers that had been built around me. Through introspection's looking glass, I pieced together my narrative's mosaic, each shard colored by my history, struggles, and epiphanies. Lifting the veil of silence, the chorus of my dialogue emerged resonant and true, the clarion testament to my very essence. The process of self-discovery was a journey of both pain and triumph, a reclamation of the self that had been long buried.

My unearthed voice was an unveiled soul stepping into the light of its own destiny, seen, heard, and irrepressibly alive. I became a cartographer of my vocal landscape, mapping my truths, and navigating the crests and troughs of innermost reverberations. My worthiness propelled me forward to realms where my declarations were met not with contempt but with the dignity of respect and understanding. The act of speaking my truth became a sacred ritual, a way to honor the journey that had brought me to this moment.

In the heart of self-confrontation, my dialogue echoed between yesterday's wounds and today's wisdom. With every reverberation through the ruins, a deeper cognizance burgeoned - these shadows no longer commanded authority. The emerging self-reclaimed, whittling away the vestiges of muted resignation. The process of healing was a dance between light and shadow, a constant negotiation between the past and the present.

As the hush lifted, my story became a mosaic where pieces of broken silence assembled into a testament of resilience. Speaking out was quintessentially a threshold beyond the precipice of silence to where truth stood undaunted. This utterance was liberation's melody - not a siren of anguish, but a ballad of emancipation inviting a waltz to the rhythms of honesty and solace. The act of sharing my story became a revolutionary act, a declaration of independence from the chains of silence.

Amidst disclosure's chasm, a sanctuary fashioned from once-stifled voices' stones. For every soul arising to break its quietude, another heard the call and found solace in shared strength. My voice, journeying through the valley of shadows, carried hope's luminescence, promising with each disclosure the night yawned less vast, and the stars gleamed brighter. The power of community, of shared experience, became a guiding light on my path toward healing.

To carry this spirit into brimming light was to stand at the helm where waters grew serene and support's compass was paramount. In partnership with those navigating similar waters, lanterns of kinship bolstered each other in tribulation's fog. Unity's lighthouse - the support of unwavering allies and wise guides - emerged as the cornerstone of rejuvenation on this voyage to wholeness. The journey towards healing was not one to be undertaken alone, but hand in hand with those who understood the depths of my struggle.

I became the architect of my own peace, built on learned lessons and hard-won insights. Boundaries became the bulwark of my vessel, each plank declaring self-worth, each nail asserting autonomy. They rose not as barricades but as gracious demarcations, silent sentinels over the wellspring of the inner sanctum, manifest expressions of deepest values protecting and cultivating the sense of self. The act of setting boundaries became a way to honor my own worth, to declare my right to exist on my own terms.

With newfound strength, I shared my story, finding empowerment in truth. My unwavering spirit and resilience carried me from darkness to light. With each step, I reclaimed my silenced voice, a testament to the power of the human spirit. My journey, though fraught with pain and betrayal, was ultimately one of reclamation, hope, and triumph. In speaking my truth, I became a beacon for others, guiding them toward their own transformative voyages of healing and self-discovery. The legacy of my journey was not only my own healing, but the countless lives I touched along the way, a ripple effect of hope and resilience that would continue to inspire for generations to come.

About Stephanie Walker

Stephanie Walker, a native of Columbia, South Carolina, is the proud mother of her only child, Tyler Scott. She has been married to Samuel Walker for eight years and they currently reside in Hephzibah, Georgia. Stephanie is a survivor of sexual violence that occurred during her childhood and adulthood. At the age of 44, she saw her predator sentenced for the first time, which empowered her to find her voice and freedom.

Through her healing journey, Stephanie made the courageous decision to transform her pain into a powerful voice speaking out against sexual violence. Unlike many survivors whose traumas are often overlooked or forgotten, Stephanie refuses to stay silent. She has become an activist, standing up for herself and others who have endured similar experiences. Stephanie is now the face and voice of the #IAMNOLONGERSILENT movement, dedicated to breaking the cycle of silence and stigma surrounding sexual violence. Through her advocacy work, Stephanie hopes to inspire others to speak out, seek help, and heal from their own traumas.

Connect with Stephanie

FB: @iamnolongersilent.walker.3

LeAnne Dolce

ABOUT LEANNE DOLCE

Meet LeAnne Dolce, PMP – a visionary, a beacon of hope, and the driving force behind the transformative Wake Up Happy, Sis! network. LeAnne is also the Founder of Wake Up Happy Sis Inc. and a Self-Care Strategist who has dedicated over 18 remarkable years to empowering high-achieving Black women. Her journey is one of resilience, transformation, and unyielding passion for fostering wellness and self-care among those who are often taught to place themselves last.

LeAnne's story is both inspiring and deeply relatable. There was a pivotal moment when she faced her own crossroads, battling depression, morbid obesity, and an overwhelming sense of defeat. It was a wake-up call that resonated with the stark reality: change or die. This personal revolution was not just about her; it mirrored the silent battles many Black women face daily. The fear that prioritizing oneself could inadvertently harm those they hold dear is a heavy burden, but LeAnne emerged as a testament to the transformative power of self-love and care.

With both Bachelors and Masters degrees in Technical Communication from the University of Washington, LeAnne's expertise spans beyond her educational achievements. She is a mother, a grandmother, and a serial entrepreneur whose career has navigated the intricate paths from corporate communications to IT Project and Program management, and ultimately to entrepreneurship. Her certifications as a Project Management Professional, wellness professional, and natural and organic product formulator only scratch the surface of her multifaceted identity. LeAnne is also a published author and a motivational speaker, whose words ignite the spark of change in the hearts of many.

At the core of LeAnne's mission [to help 1 million black women live happy, healing, and fulfilling lives unapologetically and without guilt] is the Wake Up Happy, Sis! network – a sanctuary she lovingly crafted to address the unique challenges Black women face, such as superwoman syndrome, societal pressures, workplace microaggressions, and the lingering effects of past traumas. It's a space where feminine energy is rekindled, past traumas are healed, and living a guilt-free life isn't just a dream but a tangible reality. This network fosters a nurturing environment that champions self-love, self-care, and self-development, guiding Black women from a state of merely surviving to a life of unapologetically thriving. It's more than just a community; it's a movement dedicated to reimagining self-care and wellness as essential, non-negotiable pillars for Black women seeking happiness and fulfillment.

LeAnne's role as the host of the Wake Up Happy, Sis! Show amplifies her influence, creating a platform where stories of resilience, expert advice, and personal experiences converge to inspire and guide listeners toward living their best lives personally and professionally. Her interviews shine a light on the path to wellness, offering a beacon of hope and actionable insights for those ready to embark on their healing journey.

LeAnne Dolce is not just a name; it's a legacy of empowerment, a voice for the voiceless, and a reminder that self-care is the foundation of true success. Her energy, enthusiasm, and unwavering commitment to uplifting Black women are palpable in every endeavor she undertakes. LeAnne isn't just changing lives; she's shaping a future where Black women thrive unapologetically, supported by a sisterhood that understands the importance of happiness, health, and holistic well-being.

In a world that often demands too much, LeAnne stands as a world changer, reminding us all that the act of prioritizing oneself is not just an act of survival but the highest form of rebellion against a system that expects ceaseless sacrifice. With LeAnne Dolce at the helm, the journey from surviving to thriving is not just possible; it's inevitable.

READER'S GUIDE/ DISCUSSION QUESTIONS

1. In what ways have societal expectations and stereotypes of Black women influenced your own self-perception and life choices? How can you begin to dismantle these internalized narratives and redefine your identity on your own terms?

2. Many of the women in this anthology experienced profound betrayal and abuse at the hands of those meant to protect them. How can we, as individuals and as a community, work to break cycles of intergenerational trauma and create safer spaces for healing and growth?

3. The concept of the "Strong Black Woman" is a double-edged sword, celebrating resilience while often dismissing the need for self-care and vulnerability. How can we reframe this narrative to honor strength while also normalizing and prioritizing the need for support and rest?

4. Each author's journey highlights the transformative power of self-love and self-acceptance. What are some practical steps you can take to cultivate a more loving and compassionate relationship with yourself, particularly in the face of personal challenges or societal pressures?

5. Many stories in the anthology touch on the profound impact of silence and the liberation found in speaking one's truth. In what areas

of your life might you be silencing your own voice or needs, and what would it look like to begin to break that silence?

6. The women in these stories often found strength and healing through the support of other women. How can we foster more spaces of authentic sisterhood and community care, both in our personal lives and in our broader communities?

7. Forgiveness - of others and of oneself - is a recurring theme throughout the anthology. What role does forgiveness play in your own healing journey, and how can you practice it in a way that honors your own boundaries and well-being?

8. Many authors describe a pivotal moment of choosing themselves and their own happiness, even when it meant going against familial or societal expectations. What does "choosing yourself" mean to you, and what fears or obstacles might be holding you back from fully embracing this act of self-prioritization?

9. The stories in this anthology illustrate the incredible resilience and creativity of Black women in the face of adversity. What unique strengths and wisdom have you gained from your own challenges, and how can you leverage these gifts to create positive change in your life and in the world?

10. The title "Gumbo for the Soul" evokes the idea of nourishment and sustenance. As you reflect on your own journey, what are the key ingredients you need to feel truly nourished and fulfilled - physically, emotionally, spiritually, and mentally? How can you begin to incorporate more of these elements into your daily life?

ENDORSEMENTS

This is a very well put-together anthology that showcases the amazing power of storytelling. Each story has its own unique voice, offering readers a wide range of experiences and emotions. The writing is consistently excellent, highlighting the great talent and creativity of the authors. Whether it's a touching memoir or a thought-provoking piece of fiction, these stories come together to form a vivid picture of human life that feels both personal and universal. The way the authors communicate their characters and journeys draws the reader in and creates a strong sense of connection and empathy.

What makes this anthology truly special is how each author tells their story with clear and distinct voices. Every piece is a well-crafted gem, reflecting the diverse backgrounds and perspectives of its writer. The smooth blending of different styles and voices shows the editors' great skill in selecting and organizing the stories. The authors' ability to share deep emotions and ideas with such clarity and grace is both impressive and inspiring. This isn't just a collection of stories; it's a celebration of writing and its lasting power to move, challenge, and uplift. "Gumbo for the Black Woman's Soul" is a must-read for anyone looking to be touched by the endless possibilities of human expression.

~Matilda

JOIN THE WAKE UP HAPPY SIS ACADEMY

If you've been inspired by the stories in 'Gumbo for the Black Woman's Soul,' we invite you to join us in the Wake Up Happy Sis Academy. This monthly membership community is your sacred space to learn, grow, and connect with a sisterhood of phenomenal Black women.

In the Academy, we dive deeper into the themes of resilience, self-love, and healing that are woven throughout the anthology. Through workshops, resources, and intimate discussions, we support each other in breaking free from the 'Superwoman' syndrome, healing past traumas, and embracing our authentic selves without guilt or apology.

Here, you'll find a circle of sisters who see you, hear you, and uplift you. It's a space where you can take off the mask of perfection and be embraced for the beautiful, complex, and resilient woman you are.

Join us in the **Wake Up Happy Sis Academy** and embark on a transformative journey of empowerment. Together, we'll celebrate our triumphs, navigate our challenges, and reclaim our joy, peace, and power.

Don't just survive, sis. Thrive. Join the **Wake Up Happy Sis Academy** today and embrace the life of happiness, healing, and fulfillment you deserve. We can't wait to welcome you home.

Join us at https://academy.wakeuphappysis.com. Use code 'GUMBO' to get 1 free month!

www.ingramcontent.com/pod-product-compliance
Lightning Source LLC
Chambersburg PA
CBHW051952290426
44110CB00015B/2213